# Aboriginal Spirituality and Biblical Theology:

## Closer than You Think

John W. Friesen, Ph.D., D.Min., D.R.S.

The University of Calgary

**Detselig Enterprises Ltd.**

**Calgary, Alberta, Canada**

**Aboriginal Spirituality and Biblical Theology:**
**Closer than You Think**

The University of Calgary

Canadian Cataloguing in Publication Data
Friesen, John W.
  Aboriginal spirituality and biblical theology

  Includes bibliographical references and index.
  ISBN 1-55059-209-2

  1. Indians of North America – Religion.  2. Christianity.  I. Title.
E98.R3F74  2000    299'.7    C00-9108355-1

Detselig Enterprises Ltd.
210, 1220 Kensington Road NW
Calgary, Alberta  T2N 3P5

Phone: (403) 283-0900
Fax: (403) 283-6947
email: temeron@telusplanet.net
www.temerondetselig.com

We acknowledge the financial support of the Government of Canada
through the Book Publishing Industry Development Program (BPIDP)
for our publishing activities

Cover design: David J Friesen and Alvin Choong

Printed in Canada          SAN 115-0324          ISBN 1-55059-209-2

*To my wife,*
*Virginia Lyons Friesen,*
*my partner in everything*

# Contents

## Other Detselig Titles by
## John W. Friesen

*People, Culture and Learning,* 1977

*Strangled Roots,* 1982

*Schools With a Purpose,* 1983

*When Cultures Clash: Case Studies in Multiculturalism,* 1985

*The Cultural Maze: Complex Questions on Native Destiny in Western Canada,* 1991

*When Cultures Clash: Case Studies in Multiculturalism,* Second Edition, 1993

*Pick One: A User-Friendly Guide to Religion,* 1995

*Rediscovering the First Nations of Canada,* 1997

*Sayings of the Elders: An Anthology of First Nations' Wisdom,* 1998

*First Nations of the Plains: Creative, Adaptable and Enduring,* 1999

*Legends of the Elders,* 2000

# Preface

When I first stood on the eastern shoreline of Lake Hector on the Stoney (Nakoda Sioux) Indian Reserve in Alberta some thirty years ago, I knew immediately that it was a special place. It is called a place of contemplation, of introspection and tranquility, and it certainly lives up to its name. Today Nakoda Lodge stands on that location and offers a series of restful motel rooms to guests in full view of Mount Yamnuska, the sacred mountain to the west.

Traditionally, the Stoney Indians occupied this area with a sense of awe, the same perspective with which they once viewed all aspects of nature. Like other Plains Indian Nations, they took nothing for granted, not the mountains, trees, grass, birds, fish or animals. Each living thing was perceived as capable of lending a potential assist to anyone on a spiritual quest to discover what their purpose in life might be. Living completely in tune with the rhythms and vicissitudes of nature, the Stoney People could not really conceptualize what it meant to the emerging industrial society to conquer and exploit aspects of nature in an effort to "build a better life."

Today things are different on the reserve. Although most of the topological features of the Stoney community at Morley, Alberta, remain the same, the ancient values of sharing, trust and tribal pride have for the most part been replaced by commercialism and consumerism. Fortunately, it is still possible to spend meaningful moments with some of the nation's elders and be rewarded with a vivid glimpse into the past, accompanied by a wistful longing for the old days.

During my three decade sojourn on the Stoney Reserve I have had many opportunities to learn about traditional Stoney culture from older, caring people who patiently shared insights with me about traditional tribal life. As they reminisced it became clear to me that some of them were not yet caught up in the throes of the cultural transition to modernity so evident among younger people on the reserve. These elders still revere the workings of nature and exhibit many of the old values like decision-making by consensus, living in harmony with nature and respect for individuality.

During my many discussions with elders over the years it has become clear to me that there is a great deal of similarity between the spirituality so evident among these folk and that which I had been taught about Christianity in Sunday school. This book is the result of my search thus far. As the elders might say, "Your search is never over until the Creator calls you home. Life is a journey and each day is but a step towards its fulfilment."

I wish to acknowledge a debt to the members of the congregation of Morley United Church who so graciously shepherded me to a better understanding of Stoney ways through the years that I served as their minister. There is no doubt in my mind that I learned a great deal more from them than they did from me – theologically as well as in terms of Christian practice. I only hope that in the future my life will reflect some of the fruits of the energies they extended on my behalf.

I would again like to thank my publisher, Dr. Ted Giles, and the staff of Detselig Enterprises, for supporting my work through the years. My friend, Ted, is always open to new ideas for another book and I greatly appreciate this. Our business and personal relationship has been a constant source of encouragement to me through the years.

Finally, as always, I want to thank my wife, Virginia Lyons Friesen, for her commitment as a full partner in our journey through life. Her assistance at Morley United Church as pianist, Sunday school teacher, choir director and social convenor has been invaluable, but it pales in comparison to the commitment she has shown to our mutual questing for spiritual meaning.

If there are errors in either accuracy or description in this book, they are mine, and I apologize for them. I only hope there are not too many of them, and that they do not detract from the book's central message.


J.W.F.

August 2000

The University of Calgary

# One

# The Basis for This Book

The First Nations of North America are faring a bit better in literature these days than they did a few decades ago. Brown and Vibert (1998: ix) suggest that "these are exciting and challenging times in Native history and historiography" implying that these days there is a new approach underway with regard to the examination of and writing up the past events of Aboriginal life. Many emerging historians have Native background as well as academic training, and with their writings they provide a new dimension to the interpretation of past events. This development has assisted in bringing Indian history alive with the hope that it may correct past errors in interpretation and shed new light on old mysteries.

For too long, contemporary Euro-North Americans were taught that the Indigenous Peoples of this continent did not have a history since they had not devised very sophisticated methods of writing and preserving records pertaining to events that occurred before European contact. To the contrary, however, before contact almost all social knowledge, including religious traditions and rituals that informed the Aboriginal Peoples and shaped their identities, was carried and conveyed to the next generation by oral means. As a tribal people, these folk must have had good memory banks! Symbols rich in meaning were emblazoned on animals skins, in sacred medicine bundles, and on homes, ocean-going vessels and clothing. These means of conveyance were precarious in that their sense of cultural identity and maintenance of symbolic meanings were all dependent on the degree to which they were successfully transmitted to the succeeding generations. If the bearers of knowledge died without having successfully accomplished the act of transmission, a practice or belief might be irretrievably lost (Harrod, 1995: 101).

Since cultural maintenance was such serious business, the early North American tribal societies steadfastly committed themselves to very vigorous and comprehensive pedagogical programs aimed at preserving a valued way of life. It is in large part thanks to the painstaking efforts of these dedicated and foresighted individuals that we know as much about First Nations history and culture as we do. Charles Eastman Ohiyesa (1980: 121), an elder of the Sioux Nations compared the impact of the oral tradition of his people to the importance of the Christian Bible to people of that faith:

> This Bible of ours was our whole literature, a living Book, sowed as precious seed by our wisest sages, and springing anew in the wondering eyes and upon the innocent lips of little children. Upon its hoary frost of proverb and fable, its mystic and legendary lore thus sacredly preserved and transmitted from father to son, was based in large part on our customs and philosophy.

## Changing Impressions

The perception that there is much to learn from North American Indian cultures has come about slowly. The receptiveness that now prevails is in part attributable to the spiritual and cultural renaissance which blossomed in Aboriginal communities around the 1960s (Lincoln, 1985). The civil rights movement helped, of course, as did the Vietnam War and the celebration of Canada's centennial birthday. The 1960s were a time in which to ask questions in an effort to seek a redefinition of nationhood, both in the United States and in Canada. As the intensity of questions mounted, the search for answers gained equal momentum. What, if any, was the purpose of the Vietnam War? What were the issues to which Black Power addressed itself? What was Canada going to do with the next one hundred years? What role would the First Nations play in the third millennium?

The turning point toward investigating and perhaps appreciating Indian beliefs has followed a long road, and its slow beginnings are well illustrated in a story about Joe Dion related by Pettipas (1994: 202). Dion, a Cree elder, once became very exasperated in a situation in which he was trying to defend Native traditions before a group of sceptical non-Natives and he said so. "Poor overbearing palefaces" he stated, "you have so much to learn from the Indian. Had you taken the trouble . . . to come off your high horse." The high horse, it seems, had many dimensions, including a low assessment of Native spiritual beliefs which were often ascribed labels of belittlement; they were described as "foolish, unreasonable, heathen, misguided, irrational, emotional" (Pettipas, 1994: 23) and "one of the lowest forms of religion" (MacLean, 1980: 439).

Tooker (1979: 20) points out that the first American anthropologists to sponsor indepth studies of First Nations had some difficulty with objectivity when it came to describing Aboriginal spirituality. Edward B. Tylor (Tooker, 1979: 21), for example, suggested that the Aboriginal Peoples operated in accordance with a minimal kind of religion because they believed in a universe occupied by spiritual beings. He coined the word "animism" to describe their faith system and suggested that it characterized nations who were very low on the scale of humanity. Because Native People believed that communication with the spirits of a variety of phenomena was possible, the word animism was also applied to trees, sun, moon, stars, thunder, stones and objects of material culture like kettles, pipes, and so on. Obviously influenced by the thinking of their European forebears, social scientists like Tyler and his peers perceived of First Nations' spirituality as "a pure, naive worship of nature" (Tooker, 1979: 21).

The first European missionaries who came to Indian country believed they were entrusted with "sacred truth," compared to the "mythological beliefs" of the First Nations. They found it inconceivable to consider that the two systems of thought could in any way be perceived as being of equal validity. In one instance when a missionary was being enlightened about traditional Indian truths, he quickly dismissed what had been told him with a flippant remark. His Aboriginal informant then responded in a fashion that revealed the true nature of the insult.

> "My brother," gravely replied the offended Indian. "It seems that you have not been well grounded in the rules of civility. You saw that we who practice these rules, believed your stories; why, then, do you refuse to credit ours?" (Eastman, 1980: 121)

Not only were Aboriginal beliefs and practices discredited, they were also targeted for transformation. Many missionaries quickly dismissed Indian theology as fallacious, heathen and in desperate need of replacement. A few of their peers who managed to give the Indian way of thinking more than a passing glance seized upon the idea that if First Nations' metaphysics possessed any semblance of validity, it must be similar in structure to that held by the invaders. The incoming enlightened spiritual leaders then tried to superimpose the paradigm of European thought on the unsuspecting Aboriginals and belabored them with notions of monotheism and polytheism, Calvinism and Arminianism, transcendence and immanence, and good and evil. The apparent distinctions of these refined notions, notably monotheism and polytheism, served to confuse the Natives who only had the Creator in view as the ultimate object of their worship. The spirits which occupied the realm of humankind could be viewed as teachers with whom one could communicate and perhaps appease on occasion, but only the Creator was worshipped. The confusion was further perpetuated when the newcomers introduced a form of spiritual dualism which postulated a good spirit with a legion of angels on the one hand, and the evil one with his swarm of fiends on the other. This represented the world not as a unity but as an arena of unending conflict between good and evil (Spence, 1994: 104).

It is only recently that non-Native theologians have begun to realize that the First Nations did practice a vital and living theology at the time of first contact and its foundations are still very much in place. Harrod (1995: 30) describes the role that theology played in precontact Native cultures;

> Religion was an essential ingredient in the creation and maintenance of the social identities of all these peoples, and religious energies were foundational in the construction of new social realities as they responded to either imposed or chosen alterations in their environment.

Some of the characteristics of Aboriginal spirituality did not exactly parallel those of the incoming Europeans, but that realization should not have thrown investigators off completely. What was at fault was their outlook, their uncompromising sense of mission. They came to teach and command, not to listen and learn. Had they investigated they might have discovered that the First Nations had a strong faith, but no missionaries. They were not spiritual imperialists, nor was their thinking affected by the protestant work ethic or keeping up with the Jones'. They did not have to "work out their salvation [on others] by fear and trembling" (Philippians 2:12b KJV). Their traditions revolved instead around seeking fulfilment in life and communicating with the various manifestations of creation in order to realize a higher level of completeness in their life's journey.

Cajete (1994: 43f), a Tewa Indian and member of Santa Clara Pueblo in New Mexico, describes American Indian spiritual orientation as having five unique characteristics. Since these beliefs had no easy parallel with the major elements of European systems, some confusion might have temporarily stymied even the most serious investigator who at the time of first contact sought to understand it.

The first characteristic of First Nations theology is its inherent, yet undisclosed, complexity. The Indigenous Peoples did not elaborate a minutely delineated set of doctrines, but lived them out and passed them on in principle via the oral tradition and by example. Cajete (1994: 43) suggests that the traditional First Nations' metaphysical belief system did not adhere to an overall, organized description. It was a way of life, not a carefully cataloged delineation of major and minor doctrines, subdoctrines and corollary beliefs. Theology, to the Aboriginal, was a process rather than an intellectual structure. This perspective was paralleled to some extent in the 1960s when liberation theologians challenged the academic stance of ivory tower intellectuals to stop debating the existence of God with atheists and join forces with the oppressed and down-trodden in society. Together they could engage in the struggle for social and economic equity. Like their First Nations counterparts who lived some centuries earlier, the theologians of the 1960s believed that if God is real, then He must be involved in the struggles of the present to bring about liberation from oppression (Grenz and Olson, 1992: 201).

Secondly, the spiritual stance of the First Peoples was premised on the idea that words and language have a quality of spirit because they can be an expression of the human soul. Language as prayer and song has an energy in its own dimension and can influence other energies toward certain ends. As pointed out earlier, anthropologists who failed to understand this force labelled it animism.

The third unique feature of Aboriginal religion was the belief that anything created with spiritual intent originated with that act a unique quality and spiritual power that should be respected. Art, therefore, as the result of a creative process, became deserving of respect.

The fourth characteristic was the perspective that the universe moves in never-ending invisible cycles of creation. Knowledge of the cycles (though partial), was used to structure and express the sacred in the communal context of traditional Indian life.

Finally, there was in place the understanding that Nature is the true ground of spirituality. Father Creator and Mother Earth together provide for humankind, their children. The appropriate response on the part of their offspring should be the grateful acknowledgement that everything in the universe is a sacred and spiritual gift.

As the world continues to shrink and global concerns become dinner table talk, awareness of and tolerance towards cultural differences have also heightened. There are many encouraging signs: religious denominations that once viewed one another with suspicion are cooperating on certain fronts. Leaders of the Roman Catholic Church and the Orthodox Church, for example, met for talks in 1999, the first time this has happened since the Great Schism that drove them apart. In March 2000, Pope John Paul II issued an apology to the nations of the world that had been abused and oppressed by the Church through the centuries. Today Roman Catholic and Anglican leaders in Canada are discussing mutual theological concerns. Although there are other signs of a growing concern on the part of the Christian community for interchurch cooperation, it is probably too soon to say that the world is getting to be a better place to live. Such a view is probably optimistic.

Sadly, the deeper sensitivity and softer stance toward distinctive cultural practices has probably not been influenced as much by a changing theology as it has been by increased travel, enhanced media awareness and a more widely-read public. These factors have sparked a greater interest in the spiritual and cultural beliefs of the First Nations of North America, much of it quite healthy. There are those who cannot help but exhibit a condescending tone when addressing topics pertaining to alternate metaphysical systems, obviously emanating from a lack of experience in intercultural matters or a failure to comprehend the implications of significant cultural practices. Overall, however, it is probably safe to say that in many ways the various cultures of North America are coming together. North Americans are beginning to discover cultural universals instead of dwelling on differences. In some ways it might even be conjectured that a kind of universal philosophy of caring is evolving, partially attributable to a public awareness regarding what members of the human race have been doing to the earth.

MaGaa (1990: 204) has sketched four traditional value themes of Native spirituality which might well summarize the basic tenets of this new worldview: (i) respect for the Creator, which parallels the rising interest in spiritual matters; (ii) respect for Mother Earth, that is, global concerns; (iii) respect for our fellow man and woman in the sense of seeking equity for peoples of all backgrounds particularly in the realm of health, education and welfare; and (iv) respect for individual freedom pertaining to religion, politics and lifestyle.

Porterfield (1990: 154f) contends that the American Indian spirituality movement is a form of counterculture based on several remarkably similar beliefs. The universally agreed upon tenets of Indian theology include condemnation of EuroAmerican exploitation and mistreatment of the First Nations with the parallel contention that precolonial America was made up of people who respected the earth as a place where nature and humanity should live together in peace and harmony. The common worldview of contemporary Indian spiritualists is that this attitude must be rekindled. Hence, the emphasis today is not so much on reviving ancient beliefs, rituals and traditions but on finding ways to influence and transform the culture of dominant society in terms of Indian values. An illustration of this was Sioux elder, Black Elk's attempt to equate the Great Spirit with the God worshipped by European missionaries. As Black Elk put it, "when Christians learn to appreciate the rituals that centre on the sacred pipe of peace, then they will realize that we Indians know the One true God, and that we pray to Him continually" (Porterfield, 1990: 159).

Contemporary theologians have enlarged the parameters of their pursuits by delving into aspects of religious thought heretofore only glossed over, such as Black liberation theology, Latin American theology, feminist theology, and so on. As Klein, Blomberg and Hubbard (1993: 457) state,

> We must take the time to listen to divergent readings of Scripture from our Christian brothers and sisters around the globe, and particularly from women, minorities, and the poor. As we do so, we will be both convinced and renewed.

North American theologians are daring to investigate ancient sacred assertions about transcendence and immanence without necessarily appealing to spatial categories. Medieval thinkers posited that God dwells in the heavens above but nevertheless is present in the world below. Contemporary theologians are daring to conjecture that such a balance may not be the only valid means of viewing the universe (Grenz and Olson, 1992: 310). They are seriously investigating the Aboriginal notion that the universe is one unified, interconnected entity. As the tension between immanence and transcendence mounts it may be possible to slip some Aboriginal conceptualizations of the universe into the dialogue without being severely criticized or even scorned. Evidently, meaningful conversations along these lines are now possible.

## The Urge to Write

This book is intended to be an eye-opener for those who know little about Aboriginal spirituality. I have discovered in my own journey that there is really only one way to learn about Native spirituality and that is to participate in its rituals through the arena of field work. Fortunately, friends in Indian country have been kind and have extended many invitations to me to participate in spiritual ceremonies. The journey to date has been worth it; I have certainly learned there are no short-cuts to gaining this knowledge, and as the elders might say, "life is a journey that cannot be travelled in a weekend."

My own travels have taken me a considerable way, including birth and childhood in northern Saskatchewan, studies in western Canada and in the midwestern United States, and a teaching career that afforded me many rich experiences in several different First Nations communities. Through the University of Calgary's Native Outreach Program I have had the privilege of working with students at Old Sun College (Blackfoot), Chipewyan and Woodland Cree (Fort Chipewyan Extension Program), Plains Cree (Maskwachees Cultural College), and Stoney (Nakoda Institute).

While growing up in a Mennonite community near Duck Lake, Saskatchewan, I had opportunity to attend school with Métis children in the Lac Cheval School District, although Status Indian children were bussed to St. Michael's Residential School at Duck Lake. The fact that interaction with Indian children was "off limits" served to heighten my intrigue with First Nations' cultures and I spent as much time as possible trying to learn about their ways. During harvest several families in our district hired help from the nearby reserve on a part-time basis and this gave me opportunity to engage the working men in conversation. I was an eager student and I had kind teachers. I was always trying to gain additional insights into what I considered to be an contrasting albeit fascinating lifestyle when compared to my own background.

When I arrived on the campus of the University of Calgary in 1967, a colleague and I tried to encourage our peers in the Department of Educational Foundations to offer a course in intercultural education with a focus on Native culture in Canada. We were informed that we could offer the course during weekends, and although students would be given credit for their participation, the administration would not consider the program as part of our teaching responsibilities. In other words, we would not be paid for our efforts. Ten students initially enrolled in the first term, including Vivian Ayoungman from the Siksika Nation, the first Aboriginal student to graduate from the University of Calgary. Later she went on to earn a doctorate from Arizona State University and today serves as Director of Education for the Treaty Seven organization.

As time went by, student enrolment grew and course offerings were expanded until the winter semester in 2000 when the Faculty of Education decided to eliminate any offerings in the field at the undergraduate level. Fortunately, other faculties have maintained this interest and it is now possible to complete a minor in First Nations' studies towards a bachelor's degree at the University of Calgary.

From 1970 to 1985 students who participated in the basic course on Native education were required each spring to spend a Friday night and Saturday on the Stoney Indian Reserve for a special workshop taught by the teachers of Morley Community School. The Reverend Dr. John Snow, Chief of the Wesley Band of the Stoney Nation, worked with the local conference committee and addressed the group each year on cultural and spiritual matters. Then, in 1985, the University of Calgary ruled that the weekend workshop could not be made compulsory for students and it had to be discontinued. As an alternative approach to the challenge, the Multicultural Education Council of the Alberta Teachers' Association attempted to provide relevant conferences for teachers with a special arrangement for students to participate with a nominal registration fee.

After spending two decades visiting and researching on the Stoney Indian Reserve, in 1986 I was invited to serve the community as Minister of Morley United Church. Having had ample theological training and ministerial experience, I welcomed the opportunity for two reasons; first, because I had always served in that role in a variety of denominations and, second, the invitation gave me opportunity to expand the parameters of my vision to another sphere. The plan was that my wife and I would serve in the ministerial capacity on a temporary basis until a permanent replacement could be found. The arrangement stretched out to fourteen years during which time I relied on my community informants to teach me about Stoney culture. They obliged happily and I soon discovered that my parish turned out to be an excellent laboratory from which to obtain additional subject matter for my teaching responsibilities at the university. I spent many hours with friends who served in the various capacities – chiefs, tribal councillors, teachers and elders – and all of them were very helpful in walking me through the various facets of their cultural life. I was invited to participate in a variety of rituals and regarded each invitation as a spiritual privilege – sweetgrass, pipe ceremonies, talking circles, sweat-lodge, and so on. I owe a great deal to my friends at Morley.

One of the greatest privileges for me has been to offer a course on the history of Plains Indians, particularly to Aboriginal students who have not previously had opportunity to learn about their own heritage. During the course I usually consult with these students privately and try to discover from them what they would like to have emphasized in the course. On many occasions the students have also shared with me insights about their own tribal affiliation and I have tried to incorporate these perceptions into the course with sensitivity. So far this reciprocal process has functioned well, and I look forward to maintaining it well into the future.

In 1999 my book, *First Nations of the Plains: Creative, Adaptable and Enduring* (Detselig) was published, in preparation for which my wife and I attempted to visit every Plains Indian reserve (the American term is reservation) between Alberta and Texas. It took five years of "vacations" to achieve our goal, and we only missed two reservations – the Wind River Reservation (Arapaho and Shoshone) at Lander, Wyoming and the Rosebud Reservation (Sioux) in South Dakota. We also made personal contact with friends on a number of reserves in Saskatchewan and Manitoba, and as a corollary benefit, undertook nearly a dozen trips to the southwest where we were guests at all nineteen Indian pueblos in New Mexico. Studying the lifestyle and cultural transformations of the Anazasi (the Ancient Ones), Hohokam (the Vanished Ones), and Mogollon (the Mountain People), added a special element of wonderment to the research.

During the course of these sojourns it became clear to me that the First Nations of this continent have an amazing history and they foster durable, yet flexible cultures. They represent a very old way of life, which is at the same time creative and adaptable and, above all, deeply spiritual. When assessing the various facets of my journey thus far I reached the conclusion that it was from the Crees that I learned what it means to be friendly and forgiving (especially to the Europeans who invaded their sacred territories). From the Blackfoot I learned about cultural pride. The Chipewyans taught me how to survive in the rugged north.The Stoneys taught me to believe in prayer. As time went on I became increasingly aware of my own spiritual journey and in an effort to "get it together," sought to incorporate my learnings in Indian country into the repertoire of my own Mennonite cultural heritage. As a graduate of several religious institutions where the Bible and religion were taught, it occurred to me that there was a remarkable parallel between what I had learned at home as a child and as a student in college, and what I was experiencing in First Nations' country. The language was slightly different, but most topics dealing with matters of faith, rituals and ceremonies, prayer and basic conceptualizations had a familiar ring to them. In many ways these resembled the content of the catechism I had learned in Sunday school, but I had also been given to believe that Indians adhered to a form of belief that could not be classified as theologically legitimate. I have discovered that this is a misrepresentation of Aboriginal theology, and I no longer believe it. I only wish more Christians would ease up on denunciating other faiths such as that of the Indigenous Peoples, and broaden their horizons a little. This book is dedicated towards that end.

## Plan of the Study

According to anthropologists, in the beginning civilizations usually began as tribal cultures but many transformed themselves or yielded to outside influences and developed forms of statehood. Others, like the First Nations of North America, resisted outside pressures and for several centuries practised elements of their tribal customs and beliefs in secret. The degree of cultural absorption naturally varied with each tribe, but despite outside pressures, many have retained a great deal of their ancient lore and beliefs. The cultural milieu of Plains Indians comprises a particularly rich mother lode of knowledge in this regard, despite the fact that it has required much hard work on the part of tribal leaders to enable this. It would probably not be too presumptuous to suggest that the core theological values of the Indigenous Peoples remain intact today, at least in terms of unspoken creed and ritual if not in daily practice. Like Christians, the Aboriginal Peoples often face the difficult challenge of trying not to make too many claims about their faith without living up to them.

Like other world religions, Christianity as we know it evolved from an earlier form, in this case from Judaism, itself a tribal culture in its original stages. A comparison of Hebrew tribal culture with that of the Aboriginal Peoples will reveal a great deal of similarity in belief and practice, a realization, I am sure that is not without precedent. The surprise occurs when the historical grounding of Christianity in Judaism is studied only to reveal that Christianity does not displace but builds on key theological concepts inherent in Judaism. Logically, then, it should not be surprising to note that if the theology of First Nations in its tribal form bore resemblance to that of the Hebrews, it would also have much in common with Christianity. This, indeed, is the case.

A note of caution must be sounded at the outset of this discussion, and this is to do with the observation that Native cultures are currently in a period of transition. Their traditional values are not necessarily visible in the form they once were, and their cultural transformation from tribal culture to a form of statehood, with some exceptions, has not fully materialized. As it is, elements of the dominant lifestyle in North America have been adopted by some tribes to some degree, but, as will be demonstrated throughout this book, not necessarily with a great deal of consistency and not always in the manner one might expect. About the most significant statement that may be made is that the First Nations of North America are in cultural transition and only the future will tell what direction each Indian nation will choose for itself.

The values, ceremonies and beliefs pertaining to AmerIndians discussed here pertain to their classic period of tribal configuration in which form they parallelled the Hebrew model. While the First Nations cultures remained unaffected by European impact, their theology was founded on a wholistic view of the universe and it was functional and appropriate to their times. They were a spiritual people, but not really religious in the sense that they devoted their utmost energies towards fulfilling their cosmic callings with little regard to any other obligations. Being "religious" can mean that some individuals will be so sincere about things that they work hard at what they perceive to be worthwhile – with or without any theistic acknowledgement. By contrast the Indian Peoples believed that every act and in every living thing there could be spiritual implications. One could never be sure where one might gain an insight or learn a lesson approved by the Great Spirit for one's personal journey.

The price of cultural transition is often high, particularly so in the case of the First Nations of North America. Adjustments to a rapidly urbanizing society have forced Native people to migrate to the cities in search of housing and employment, only to encounter severe discrimination and racism. A return to reserve life is often a return to poverty because the economic base on most reserves is not sufficient to accommodate the rapidly growing population. The reserve, however, offers security and acceptance; it is the place to belong. In many cases it represents a home with roots reaching back hundreds of years.

The converse of feeling at home on the reserve is the reality that many reserves suffer from excessive social problems. Suicide rates are high, as are those for alcohol consumption and drugs, and common "household" illnesses like measles, whooping cough, influenza and tuberculosis still prevail. School dropout and failure rates are also excessive, and although an increasing number of Indian youth are finishing high school and enrolling at postsecondary institutions of learning, the proportion of their numbers compared to that of the national average is still low. In addition, the number of Native individuals incarcerated in prisons per capita is high compared to the general population, and many of their violations are alcohol-related. Finally, while it is encouraging to note that infant mortality rates in Native communities have declined in recent years and life expectancy has increased, both have a long way to go to match that of dominant North American society. As if the foregoing were not enough Howard Adams (1999) insists that the domination and exploitation of Native peoples is often perpetuated from within – by corrupt Indian governments. He insists that many chiefs and councils operate to keep a semiapartheid system of government in operation that keeps power and economic control in the hands of a select few. He notes that the actual day to day corruption of the money managers is evident in the way reserve resources are used. He suggests that those in power tend to use their offices as a tool for doling out

daily oppression, impoverishment and distress on women, children and powerless individuals living on reserves. There is no denial that the government grant of six and one-half million dollars a year to First Nations reserves, does not go to the general population of residents on the reserves, nor does it benefit them. This is very typical of Third World colonial admin-istration. (Adams, 1999: 126)

As the transition from tribal culture to workable forms of third millenni-um institutionalization continues, band councils must struggle to find some solution to the problems cited above, principally improved housing, and better health programs, more education and fuller employment. A decade ago, some bands began to administer the full range of available services to their people, with the larger bands employing several hundred people as teachers, adminis-trators, accountants, social workers, office workers, carpenters, maintenance workers, and so on. Some bands also developed court systems that would take into account the Native way of doing things, that is, using a tribunal of elders to assess the form of punishment to be meted out, and identifying "peacemak-ers," who would attempt to settle arguments on site instead of referring cases to the police. A few reserves with private resources have met the challenge of being located near towns with citizens who do not have reputations for treat-ing them fairly, by setting up competing businesses in their own communities. In addition to manufacturing they have started restaurants, shopping centres, service stations, banks, and so on (Buckley, 1992: 126f).

Despite experiencing some progress along the lines of effective reserve self-government, a series of old constraints may hinder Indian governments from making economic headway in the new millennium. One of the difficul-ties is that the federal government has assigned low priority to the concept of developing industries on reserves based on the assumption that very few skilled or motivated workers reside in Indian communities. Many programs that have been supported by government funding have failed, partly due to inadequate funding and government resistance to developing functional job training programs. In addition, after years of surviving under the cloud of gov-ernment dependency, it has been very hard for First Nations to shift to a mode of independence. This uncertainty has been greatly aided by the reality that Indian people for the most part have been excluded from mainstream societal decision-making and their self-confidence has been greatly weakened. The lin-gering dialog between government officials and Indian leaders to come to an agreement as to what Indian Aboriginal self-government means has served as a black cloud over First Nations' plans for future development. How can Native leaders be expected to formalize and initiate a workable plan for self-government when those who currently hold the reins of control are reluctant even to discuss the matter honestly?

## The Challenge

The bottom line for a successful future for First Nations rests to a great extent on public opinion. The lack of knowledge of Indian history, cultural structure and spirituality on the part of the public is still obvious, to say the least. At the same time, however, there is genuine interest on the part of many to learn more about traditional Aboriginal ways, and efforts to alleviate this ignorance are emerging in some quarters. Courses dealing with First Nations history and culture at the University of Calgary, for example, are well subscribed, as is the case in other such institutions. Many universities across North America in recent decades have developed departments and institutes of North American Indian Studies. The Calgary Police Service recently experimented with a three-day workshop for officers to learn more about Native spirituality on the Tsuu T'ina Reserve, and even though the program was operated on a volunteer basis, it was always oversubscribed. The media are also awakening to the reality that Aboriginal cultures have much to offer by way of program content, even if only to lend credence to already tired story plots.

Despite these encouraging signs, most Canadians probably do not know the difference between a Status Indian and a non-Status Indian or a Treaty Indian and non-Treaty Indian, and they likely could not describe the principal features of the Indian Act, Bill C-31, or the ten major treaties signed in Canada with the First Nations beginning in 1871. They would also be unaware that an eleventh treaty was signed in the Northwest Territories in 1921. Canadians would likely be joined in their ignorance by their fellow Americans in trying to explain why many Indigenous Peoples now prefer to live on reservations when they were once confined there against their will. Many North Americans have probably never been on an Indian reserve except to drive through it as a short-cut on their way to somewhere else. When they have stopped to shop or ask directions they have likely done so from the perspective of visiting a human museum, unaware of the richness and magnitude of cultures represented by the local residents.

These observations are not intended to cast a negative aura on anyone, circumstances being what they are. The stifling of Aboriginal cultural life over the last several centuries was probably enacted on the basis of impatience, misinformation and perhaps even good intentions. Governments did shirk their responsibilities when they transferred the control of Native education over to religious denominations, but religious educators for the most part thought they had the Indians' best interests at heart when they sought to "Christianize, educate and civilize" them. They were operating on the mandate that unless they carried out their marching orders, the First Nations would be robbed of their opportunity to adopt Christianity. Now, in retrospect, we can see that they were too hasty. With the possibility of a few exceptions, very few exceptions, most of the invading Europeans came to North America to conquer, capture and exploit the resources they discovered – including human resources. In rare cases, a few observers of Native culture, anthropologists or missionaries, were able to see past the agenda of cultural transformation and begin to appreciate the deeper spiritual meanings within the Aboriginal cultural milieu. If their search had been magnified to the point of influencing the majority of the newcomers, the search to understand the mysteries of Aboriginal metaphysics might have come about much sooner. As it is, all we have is today and today is a fine place to start.

## Comments on Terminology

There are some encouraging indications that the enamor with political correctness as an end in itself is waning. Still, it may be a bit risky to try to define relevant terms to everyone's satisfaction. Against this background, this risk will still be taken here in the interest of trying to keep the lines of communication open. Naturally, there are a variety of terms to choose from in writing about the original occupants of this continent – Aboriginal Peoples, AmerIndians, First Nations, First Peoples, Indians, Indigenous Peoples, Native People, North American Indians, and so on. There are also writers, Native and non-Native, who prefer a particular usage to the exclusion of all the others. In the USA, for example, the term Indian is still widely used. Canada, on the other hand, appears to have opted for First Nations or Aboriginal People. Despite arguments to the contrary, and perhaps a few will be proffered by reviewers, a variety of these terms will be employed in the ensuing pages, partly to relieve monotony in writing style, and partly because it is difficult to know which usage might be appropriate in a given context. In addition, words to describe the First Peoples will be capitalized as a means of emphasizing the literary legitimacy of writing about the AmerIndians – in the same way that identities of other nationalities are capitalized – American, Dutch, English, French, German, Polish, Spanish, Ukrainian, and so on.

In discussions about this topic with Pete Standing Alone, an Elder from the Blood Tribe, he simply said to me that it makes little difference what people call him; he grew up an Indian and he would probably remain an Indian until his death. "Words do not matter," he said, "It's what's in your heart that counts." So be it.

## The Matter of Perspective

This book will have little value for anyone who finds it difficult to believe that the spirituality of AmerIndians can rightfully take its place alongside other recognized theological, metaphysical world-views. The Indigenous way is an authentic lifestyle that begs for a closer examination of its basic premises and operation. The Aboriginal perspective is inclusive and comprehensive and, like other such systems, comprises a full contingent of philosophical subsections and fundamental corollary domains. One must not be derailed by the fact that these insights were carried and transmitted for generations via the oral tradition. Aboriginal theology is at once an intriguing, wholistic and sustaining perspective.

The arguments projected in this book are not likely to change anyone's mind unless they are perceived as a possible source of enrichment. This will hopefully be the case for those who do not place restrictions on the nature of possible sources of new knowledge – particularly when they emanate from the sector of discussions about First Nations' thinking. The reader must take the risk of trying to think differently.

This book seeks to fill a void in the literature about AmerIndian people by venturing a plain-speaking version of the fundamental premises of Plains Indian spirituality. Its basic thesis is supplemented by the realization that this information is being presented by a non-Native individual. Such an undertaking is necessarily accompanied by a certain element of risk, and this reality may subject the book's contents to a bit of healthy analysis by both Indian and non-Indian critics. With this writing I admit to having been very much influenced in my thinking by my interactions with members of the Stoney (Nakoda Sioux) Tribe at Morley, Alberta, and I herewith acknowledge a heavy debt to them. Many of the Stoneys have been very helpful and patient and kind in sharing valuable information with me about their way of life. They deserve a very special thanks. In addition, my experiences in other Indian communities must also be acknowledged. If the contents of this book in any way do justice to the elucidation of fundamental Aboriginal ways, I hope this affords honor to the respective tribes – which they much deserve.

# Two

# The Quagmire of Writing about First Nations

Native identity is coming of age in North America for the first time since the European invasion. News stories concerning the activities of First Nations are increasingly in the public eye, and the practice of Aboriginal religious ceremonies and rituals in Native communities has been intensified in recent decades. Given the strengthened vision of AmerIndian leaders to expand their influence to the political arena there are ample indications that this momentum is gaining.

Native cultural and political impact is being felt on many fronts, and many North Americans are beginning to realize that it is time to play fair with the Indians. This is a far cry from the situation less than a century ago when Indian agents ignored any pleas for assistance from Aboriginal leaders. During the early part of this century, Indian ceremonies were ignored or misunderstood by the public, condemned by missionaries and outlawed by governments. This trend is not to be interpreted as suggesting that the road ahead is entirely without religious, political and social pitfalls, for indeed there will be many of those. As Deloria Jr. (1996: 47) notes,

> Respect for non-Western traditions is exceedingly difficult to achieve. . . .
> Social science, in particular anthropology, preserved information about the
> remnants of tribal cultures around the world, most particularly in North
> America, but it also promulgated the idea that these tribal cultures were of
> Stone Age achievement and represented primitive superstitions which could
> not be believed.

The reluctance of social scientists to investigate seriously the philosophical bases of Native spirituality has a deep-seated base, rooted in the days of first contact. When the Spanish and French arrived on North American soil they came for the purpose of exploitation and expansion. They were after land and other resources; they did not come to investigate alternate theories about humankind's relationship to the universe. They came to conquer, not to learn.

As Pettipas (1994: 215) points out, the government's decision to suppress Native forms of religious expression may partially be attributed to contradictions between capitalism and Indigenous kinship-based methods of producing, distributing and consuming goods. In the Indian world religious beliefs and practices were very much part of the larger cultural complex. Property sometimes exchanged hands through religious ceremonies and this was unacceptable to European mores.

Further, there was a discrepancy between the European scientific orientation to discover and endorse "facts" solely via the scientific method. That attitude still prevails among too many scientists who insist that there can only be one foundation on which further scientific discoveries can be made, and that is the one on which they are operating. A North American example of such bigoted close-mindedness has to do with the power and efficacy of prayer, a strong structural arm of Native spirituality. Sadly, this close-mindedness prevails today.

A medical practitioner for many years, Larry Dossey (1997) discovered that some patients in his care seemed to have "extra help" in getting well, and they sincerely attributed this "secret ingredient" to their faith in prayer. After serious investigation, Dossey gave up medicine to study this phenomenon. Today, his publications are well-known, and he strongly supports the power of prayer with the support of 231 empirical studies, drawn from a variety of fields such as medicine, psychology and anthropology. Dossey exonerates the traditional role of shaman, and pleads for tolerance and flexibility on the part of those who insist on filling the role of medical doctor only within the parameters of the traditional strait-jacket of traditionally-defined American medical practice. Dossey insists that sometimes, in order for people to be healed all resources must be tapped, including miracle drugs, counselling, physical manipulation (therapy) and prayer.

If Dossey's position is backed by a well-defined research methodology rendering reliable documentation, why do so many "scientifically-oriented" medical practitioners refuse to accept his conclusions? Perhaps it is because many critics of wholistic medicine would prefer to cloud the evidence with any excuses to support their disbeliefs rather than examine either the claims made by those who believe in alternative medicine, or their own discomforts with them (Dossey, 1997: 278). The reasons for assuming this inflexible stance are many and they are usually founded on the premise that western materialistic beliefs exclude the possibility of prayer-based healing. Besides, North Americans generally resist change and suffer from what Dossey calls "cognitive dissonance," which is the condition of discomfort that people feel when there is conflict between their perceptions and their belief system. They may not like what they see to be true so they refuse to accept it. The result is that shamanistic practices and unfamiliar religious practices such as prayers may conveniently be labelled "mystic," and are believed to be conducted by people who are strange or different – like Indian healers. Investigators insist that those practices would not (must not) work in our culture. In the final analysis, careers and financial investments may be at stake, forcing a reluctance on the part of stake holders to be willing to investigate or test a new approach.

According to Goulet (1998: xxxii), a northern people, the Dene Tha, do not differentiate between knowledge gained by direct experience and that derived via dreams and visions, and they have designed a procedure by which to determine a seeker's qualification for investigating their ways. Before communicating about knowledge obtained through the latter route, the Dene assess the investigator's personal experiences of such phenomena. Further information may be imparted to the seeker to the degree that he or she is deemed qualified to appreciate that knowledge. The form in which rudimentary knowledge is first imparted is via stories and the listener is directed to observe carefully what the people did and said in the tale because the teachings are in the words and actions. Only later on, when the investigator is considered ready to appropriate deeper forms of impartation can he or she expect to obtain any kind of response to a direct question. As one Dene elder observed, "We tell you these stories for you to think with, as they were given to me for me to think with" (Goulet, 1998: xxxiii).

Despite the reluctance of modern scientists to be "scientific," in the sense of being inquisitive, objective, and analytical regarding all manner of phenomena, there is evidence that some headway is being made in terms of the gradual acceptance of alternative ways of thinking, believing and acting. Some investigators may reveal little more than a shallow curiosity towards Indigenous ways, but there are some positive signs that the scientific community may be coming around. However, a caution must be sounded. If so-called "inquisitive" scientists take so long in altering their perspectives, imagine how much less hope there can be for the man/woman-on-the-street.

## Off to a Bad Start

Despite efforts to update source materials, most libraries in North America are still well-stocked with books depicting Native people in uncomplimentary and inflammatory ways. A case in point is Edwin Denig's diatribe against five tribes of the Upper Missouri – Arikaras, Assiniboines, Crees, Crows and Sioux, written about the middle of the last century. The book was copyrighted in 1961 by the University of Oklahoma and edited by John C. Ewers. Somewhat surprisingly, Ewers compliments Denig's racist ramblings, labelling them as written "with a high degree of objectivity." and offering, for example, "the most complete and authentic description of Assiniboine Indian culture in the middle nineteenth century known to ethnology." He cites Denig as "showing uncanny accuracy," and "being the most knowledgeable writer on Indian tribes of the Upper Missouri" (Ewers, 1961: xiii-xxxviii). After examining some of Denig's remarks, one can only wonder what "less" racist manuscripts must be like that may have been written during that period. Ewers compliments Denig for "setting the record straight regarding not only the history and ethnology of the Upper Missouri tribes, but with respect to the character of these Indians as well" (Denig, 1961: xxxi).

An examination of Denig's "objectivity" with specific regard to the Assiniboines includes his observation that despite the efforts of the American Fur Company, "It required some years to bring these wild savages to anything like order" (Denig, 1961: 70). Thanks to the American Fur Trading Company,

> By a judicious and well regulated trade, however, they have been greatly changed for the better. . . . What was once filthy skin clothing has given way before good and handsome apparel of American manufacture, which enables both sexes of all ages to appear tolerably neat and clean. (Denig, 1961: 89)

Denig goes on to condemn virtually ever aspect of the Assiniboine way of life, despite himself being married to two Assinboine women at the same time. He notes that "There are but few handsome women among them, and virtue is still a rarer commodity except in very young females" (Denig, 1961: 97). One wonders what kind of respect Denig had for his own spouses. According to his description, the Assiniboines were of a thievish and malicious disposition, and although not bloodthirsty, they made trader's lives miserable by stealing their horses, robbing and abusing the men in their employ, killing the domestic cattle of the fort, and in short, annoying them in every way. In addition, apparently the Assiniboines

> were famed for being lazy, thieving, ignorant and malicious. They had but little home regulation, governed by very precarious and insufficient laws, and did not respect the private rights of their own or any other people. (Denig, 1961: 89)

Denig also accused the Assinboines of being unconscionable beggars, who regarded every person as a source from which benefit was to be derived, caring little for anyone else but themselves. They were accused of clinging tenaciously to their old customs, refusing to keep up with the age of advancement to the same degree that other nations did who had fewer opportunities. They were allegedly so backward that when famine occurred, they devoured their horses and dogs and in some cases even their own children.

An entirely different image of First Nations may be gleaned from sources other than Edwin Denig's version, for example, a note in one of Christopher Columbus' first letters to Spain's royal court, "So tractable, so peaceable are these people, that I swear to your Majesties that there is not in the world a better nation" (Brown, 1981: 1). Columbus' impressions were paralleled by other newcomers, for example, that of missionary, Father A. M. Beede, who described the Sioux (parent nation of the Assiniboines), as a "true church of

God" with a religion of truth and kindness. He suggested that the Sioux had no need for a missionary so he abandoned the role and devoted his life to the study of law so he could help the Sioux in the capacity of legal adviser. He was defrocked by the church, of course, and spent the rest of his life in service to "the downtrodden race of America" (Seton and Seton, 1966: 38). Father Wilhelm Schmidt supplemented Beede's observations by careful analysis of the theological system of various Indigenous Peoples, and argued that there were no grounds on which to label their beliefs as less valid than those emanating from Europe. Schmidt vigorously propounded the theory that at the time of the first arrival of the Europeans, the First Nations had in place a monotheistic theological system that paralleled in sophistication and complexity any system imported from across the ocean (Schmidt, 1965: 21-33).

Of Assiniboine extraction, John Snow, Chief of the Wesley Band of the Stoney Nation (Nakoda Sioux), observes that when the missionaries arrived in Stoney country their message was readily heeded. He conjectures that this might have been because of the similarity of beliefs between the two parties. The Stoneys perceived the Creator as a caring, healing Being whose attention could be secured by faith through prayer and fasting. The medical skills of the Stoneys reinforced their belief that the Creator's teachings and lessons would be learned by observing the universe around them. They studied the laws of nature and lived by them. In addition, the creations of the Great Spirit revealed many mysteries to the Stoneys and enhanced their respect for the earth (Snow, 1977: 7).

As the twentieth century began to unfold anthropological literature burgeoned, following the lead of French philosopher, Jean Jacques Rousseau's notion of portraying the First Peoples of North America as "noble savages." Rousseau argued that "this creature" ought to be saved as a remnant of the bygone days of pre-civilization when people were happy and carefree. According to Rousseau, the excessive use of reason had corrupted humankind and a return to the days of pre-civilization, such as that practised by the First Nations, was the only remedy for societal ills (Surtees, 1969: 90; Friesen and Boberg, 1990: 8-9).

Travelling across the western plains in 1900, George Bird Grinnell was one of few authors who left a written legacy concerning the AmerIndian peoples. Grinnell perceived that

> the Indian has the mind of a child in the body of a man. . . . his mind does not work like that of the adult white man. . . . by this I mean that it is a mind in many respects unused, and absolutely without training as regards all matters which have to do with civilized life." (Grinnell, 1900: 7-8)

Grinnell may have been correct that Aboriginal cultures thrived on a different cultural base than their European counterparts, but his ethnocentrism could not stop him from implying that European civilization was superior to that of the First Nations.

In fashion similar to Grinnell, his contemporary, John MacLean, entitled the first chapter in his 1896 book, *Native Tribes of Canada,* "Some Queer Folk." if nothing else providing an indication of how language has changed over the years. In MacLean's defence, however, he did admit that a faithful study of Indian languages and customs would compel anyone to acknowledge that ". . . underneath the blanket and coat of skin there beats a human heart . . . there is beauty, sweetness and wisdom in their traditions and courage, liberty and devotion in their lives" (MacLean, 1986: iv).

Anthropological surveys of North American Indians that followed Grinnell and MacLean slowly began to reflect a degree of respect for Native ways. One such classic first published in 1927, authored by Paul Radin and entitled, *The Story of the American Indian.* Although relatively objective in describing the various facets of AmerIndian culture, Radin could not refrain from ridiculing some elements of Aboriginal etiquette. As Radin noted,

> Etiquette, however seemed to reach its most ridiculous culmination in the case of a man's mother-in-law. Whenever possible he sat with his back to her. Not one word did he address to her nor, for that matter, did she address any to him. (Radin, 1937: 18)

In analyzing the spiritual context of the North American Indian cultures, Radin discounted the assumption that Indian peoples were theologically monotheistic. He argued that monotheism was not a valid religious perspective among AmerIndians, but rather the result of philosophical speculations by a small segment within the community, notably by shamans or priests. Radin contended that the Supreme Beings identified by these individuals was not meant to be worshipped, and in cases where they did become the object of spiritual adulation their position was quickly transformed into the highest position within a pantheistic realm (Radin, 1937).

A contemporary of Radin, anthropologist Clark Wissler, exhibited a bit more sensitivity, noting that First Nations were often accused of engaging in extreme measures when involved in war. Wissler pointed out that while the Indian way of making war might have been unique, it was certainly not as pagan as modern "civilized" wars where people are bombed ". . . from the air, mostly by raids to burn, mutilate, kill and spread terror, with no regard for age, sex or condition" (Wissler, 1966: 17). Although he may have hoped for it, Wissler did not anticipate the assimilation of AmerIndians in the near future, but emphasized that they should be respected for the specialized knowledge they had accumulated, such as the domestication of wild plants. He conceded that this knowledge had enabled them to live on this continent for thousands of years. Wissler's contemporary, Diamond Jenness, traversed Canadian soil from east to west, and to the far north, writing about Native people, optimistically speculating, among other things, that someday the Eskimo race, for example, would amalgamate ". . . with white trappers and traders and produce the hardy and resourceful stock necessary for the development of Canada's far North" (Jenness, 1986: 422).

As anthropologists gradually eliminated inadvertent ethnocentric comments while studying First Nations' cultures, they began to produce works more readily oriented towards the acknowledgment of Indian contributions to the North American way of life. Many, however, like Ruth Underhill (1953), still clung tenaciously to the theory that the Indigenous Peoples migrated to North American via the Bering Strait. Driver was more hesitant; "Although we are certain that there was some contact between South Pacific Islands and South America before 1492, this came much too late to account for any principal peopling of the New World" (Driver, 1968: 4).

The lack of information about the fabled Bering Strait theory did not keep anthropologists from guessing about Native origins on this continent, and they had plenty of company. The general presupposition on which the Bering Strait theory was promulgated was that since archeological evidence exists to identify the presence of Indigenous peoples 11 000 years ago in the Valley of Mexico, this means that their ancestors must have come to America via the Bering Strait thousands of years earlier. Today, anyone reading Vine Deloria, Jr.'s sarcastic repudiation of that theory is sure to agree with him that "the Bering Strait theory is simply shorthand scientific language for, 'I don't know, but it sounds good and no one will check'" (Deloria, 1995: 81). Sadly, if Deloria is correct, the most compelling reason for advancing the theory is to justify European colonization. If it can convincingly be argued that First Nations were also recent immigrants to North America, they would lose their claim to being original inhabitants and with that the right of first occupancy.

By the 1960s generic works about Indians began to take on a degree of sophistication to some extent, but musings about the Bering Strait lingered. As Owen, Deetz and Fisher indicated,

> The dates of the earliest migration to the New World are still in question. . . . Regarded as even less likely are those fanciful contentions which suggest that the origin of American Indians can be attributed to sunken continents or wandering lost tribes." (Owen, et. al., 1968: 3)

Josephy was more specific, and estimated that the bridge across the Bering Strait was probably part of the path that led to the New World some 12 000 to 35 000 years ago. Peter Farb (1968: 191) concurred, but estimated that proof existed to show that Aboriginal people had lived on this continent at least 13 000 years ago. Jennings (1978: 1) was even more persistent, insisting that "There is no reasonable doubt as to the ultimate origin of the human population that finally covered the hemisphere." There is consensus among scholars that the first American was of Asian stock." Deloria was right; for "professionals" of this ilk, any form of "educated" speculation would appear to be much superior to what they might term pure fantasy, although the differences might not be evident to anyone else.

## A New Genre

There is evidence to indicate that the tone of writing about Indian history is gradually changing, and the Aboriginal people of North America may be getting a bit of a break. Representative of the trend to provide a more balanced view is the work of Olive Dickason whose two major works shifted the attention of historians to a new slant. In Dickason's (1984) first book, *The Myth of the Savage and the Beginnings of French Colonialism in the Americas*, she investigated historical developments during European contact from the perspective of the peoples who were already resident here. The mandate perceived to be Divinely-granted to them caused the French to create an ideology that AmerIndians were savages. This description justified one of the greatest land grabs in human history as well as the squelching of the foundations of a well-established civilization. Historical accounts of the First Peoples encountered were penned by fur traders, explorers and missionaries, all of whom saw the Indigenous Peoples as inferior and just targets for exploitation. All subsequent writings were attempts to justify the imperialism of France, religious or otherwise, and permit the ruthless transcendence of all national boundaries.

As an indication of value differences between the first residents and the invaders, it should be noted that the European explorers aimed for territorial aggrandizement, unlike their Native hosts who fought for prestige, honor and booty. Radin (1937: 5) describes the extent to which chiefs were traditionally expected to serve their people:

> Try to do something for your people. . . . have pity on your people and love them. If a man is poor, help him. Give him and his family food, give them whatever they ask for. If there is discord among your people, intercede. Take your sacred pipe and walk into their midst. Die if necessary in your attempt to bring about reconciliation. Then when order had been restored and they see you lying on the ground dead, still holding in your hand the sacred pipe, the symbol of peace and reconciliation, then assuredly will they know that you have been a real chief.

First Nations sought to produce only enough food supply for their immediate or seasonal needs, and they did not hoard but shared whatever they had with anyone who had need. Their invading captors collected everything and anything in surplus amounts and placed great store on who possessed what property. A large amount of material goods was equated with spiritual prowess and assignments of stratified importance were correlated with material success. Differences such as these still persist between the world-views of Natives and non-Natives in North America, and indicate just how wide a cultural gulf is yet to be crossed if meaningful communication is to be attained.

Dickason's (1993) second book, *Canada's First Nations: A History of Founding Peoples from Earliest Times* is targeted at filling the gap of the silent years before the Europeans came. Dickason pleads for a wider scope and greater diversity of research for historians to study, other than just being document-bound. Because the First Peoples relied on an oral tradition, their recounts of past events were often ignored and much has been lost. Today, thanks to mounting archeological evidence, much of what was claimed about Native history via the oral tradition, has been substantiated. It is regrettable that a more appreciative stance for the oral tradition could not have been developed sooner so that the richness of Indian history could have been supplemented by the recorded sayings of the elders. Dickason's work combines the historical documentary approach with the oral tradition, thereby enabling her to develop a fairly complete composite of Aboriginal life in Canada before the arrival of the French.

Dickason's tack has not gone unnoticed, and definitely influenced two separate prongs of historical inquiry; first, the inclusion of First Nations' data before first contact; and, second, the provision of first-hand elder narratives to round out the program. Two books that illustrate the first influence are *Origins: Canadian History to Confederation* by Douglas Francis, Richard Jones and Donald Smith (1988), and *History of the Canadian Peoples: Beginnings to 1867* by Margaret Conrad, Alvin Finkel and Cornelius Jaenen (1993) . Although both volumes offer only single chapter outlines of Native life before the Europeans arrived, the fact of their having made the attempt to include such information shows definite improvement over earlier historical surveys. Basically, Francis and his colleagues offer one paragraph descriptions of such major themes in AmerIndian history as the moundbuilders, the buffalo, and the horse under the guise of surveying the major culture areas of Canada. Still, theirs is a noble effort in an enterprise too long neglected by North American historians.

Margaret Conrad and colleagues fare a bit better by recognizing that historians have only recently attempted to offer a fuller picture of Canadian history by going back to actual North American beginnings before the European invasion. They caution that a reverse look into our historical past could give birth to the danger of romanticizing the past life of the First Nations who were actually much like other nations in their approach to life. True, some First Nations were warlike, others had slaves, and still others engaged in wasteful hunting practices which may have caused the death of certain species of animals, but these weaknesses could easily be paralleled in other societies. These writers generously admit that until recently historians relied only on the written tradition in accumulating information about the past, and those sources were usually penned by an elite group of non-Native males who had very specific agendas.

Publications devoted solely to portraying aspects of Indian life today offer an advanced degree of sophistication and authenticity. Miller (1995: ix), for example, attempts to provide information that will build a foundation on which to answer fundamental questions about First Nations raised by the public, that is, "Just what do the Natives want?" or "Why should they have special rights in Canada?" Miller labels the colonialist policies of past governments a dismal failure and pleads for the recognition of Indian cultures and rights. The tone of his work is paralleled by Bruce Morrison and Roderick Wilson of the University of Alberta and James Frideres of the University of Calgary. Morrison and Wilson (1995: 14) build their case for a more objective look at Indigenous cultures on three assertions: (i) an understanding of Native peoples must start from an appreciation of Aboriginal society as it existed and as it continues; (ii) perceptions which Native peoples have of themselves must take into account the political dimensions of the history of relationships between Native cultures and Canadian society; and, (iii) scholars who describe the nuances of Native societies always bring an element of the subjective to the printed page. Frideres echoes these sentiments by admitting that writers who describe Aboriginal ways are often biased, and his stated purpose is to provide a critical interpretation of the "person on the street's" thinking about Native people (Frideres, 1993: viii). He succeeds in this because his approach is genuinely appreciative and indicative of a perpetual learning stance.

## Elder Stories

A very productive approach to writing First Nations' history consists of incorporating elder narratives about Native history via the oral tradition. Harrod (1995: 101) cautions that the precarious nature of the oral tradition lay in the fact that in traditional Native societies cultural identity and the maintenance of symbolic boundaries depended on continuities of social interaction. These continuities supported the rehearsal of oral traditions that fostered their ritual transmission across social time. If the bearers of that knowledge died without transmitting the meaning of these beliefs and practices to the next generation, all or part of their knowledge would be irretrievably lost. This makes current efforts to record and preserve elder stories very significant. As Eliade (1974: 509) describes this role, "It is consoling and comforting to know that a member of the community is able to see what is hidden and invisible to the rest and bring back direct and reliable information from the supernatural worlds."

One of the first published efforts to incorporate elder narratives is Marius Barbeau's *Indian Days on the Western Prairies*, first published in 1960. The work comprises a compendium of interviews with elders dating back as far as 1926. Working mainly with the Stoney Nation, Barbeau's stories include a variety of accounts including biographic sketches, descriptions of battles and vignettes of daily life on the reserve.

Ruth Kirk has undertaken a similar task among elders of the Pacific west coast tribes in a volume entitled, *Wisdom of The Elders,* 1986. Kirk describes such subjects as kinship systems, role of elders, intertribal dealings and customs of daily life, carefully weaving in personal accounts provided by elders. Similarly, Dianne Meili (*Those Who Know: Profiles of Alberta's Native Elders,* 1992) travelled across the Province of Alberta on a search for personal meaning for a year and a half, interviewing elders from more than a dozen reserves, carefully recording their community concerns and prophecies for the future. Meili's research proved to her that "many Native people still regarded elders as the powerful sources of strength and wisdom that have always been but despaired that modern society had forsaken the old ones' spiritual convictions" (Meili, 1992: ix). The elders were eager to share their stories, freely identified their concerns for the younger generations, and offered no criticisms except when it came to environmental issues. They tried to influence Meili to abandon her intensive personal search for enlightenment and allow all living things, "all her relations," to teach her love and trust.

A more global perspective of elder narratives is portrayed in Peter Knudtson and David Suzuki's *Wisdom of the Elders,* (1992) whose research took them to a multitude of civilizations in which the role of elder is still viewed with a degree of respect. Over and over again it was made clear to the authors that a radically different way of relating people to the support systems of the planet is necessary. As Suzuki notes,

> My experiences with aboriginal peoples have convinced me, both as a scientist and as an environmentalist, of the power and relevance of their knowledge and worldview in a time of imminent global ecocatastrophe. (Knudtson and Suzuki, 1992: xxxv)

The value of incorporating the wisdom of the elders into modern-day analyses of spiritual and eco-problems shows that at times their way of expressing truths is clearly more impacting than that of a more sophisticated rendition. At one point Suzuki was interviewing Paiakan, a Kayapó Indian elder from Brazil, as the two of them were touring parts of British Columbia and discussing environmental concerns. When Paiakan saw glaring evidence of clear-cutting and slash burning in the B.C. interior he noted philosophically, "People destroy the forests in Brazil because they are poor and they are ignorant. . . . What is Canada's excuse?" (Knudtson and Suzuki, 1992: xxxiii)

## Future Writings

Despite past prophecies to the contrary, most historians now agree that First Nations are here to stay. The future challenge for Native people will be to determine the structural forms their survival will take in an urbanized, aggressive, non-Native majority society. Patterson (1972: 188) suggests that the future of Indigenous peoples will likely be as fraught with threats to their survival as it has been in the past, perhaps more so, but their efforts to strengthen themselves for greater vitality, creativity and survival will obviously influence what direction their future will take. Boldt (1993: 248) identifies one of the "threats" to Aboriginal culture as the possible lack of moral will of Canadians and governments to do right by the Indians. If Canadians can remove the barriers of injustice and prejudice against Indians, and if Indians can eradicate their own social-cultural-psychological barriers to off-reserve employment, there may be hope.

As the First Nations continue to adjust to societal changes, written descriptions of their efforts will no doubt continue to appear. Social scientists probably like to think that methodologies are now in place to assure the production of accurate, non-biased renditions of AmerIndian ongoings with no fear of future embarrassment or contradiction. If those methodologies can guarantee portrayals of Indian that are indisputably accurate and fair, we will indeed be living in miracle land. What might be a poor substitute for this need could be cultural descriptions by both Native and non-Native writers, academics and non-academics, "scientifically-produced monographs" and elder narratives, produced with the hope that we, like old wine, are indeed improving with time.

# Three

# From Tribe to State:
# The Evolution of the Hebrew Nation

Adherents to Christianity are often quite unaware that their religion has distinct tribal origins not unlike those existent among the First Nations of North America before European contact. The religious forms of Christianity evolved from a culture that was once parallel in many ways to that of tribal cultures around the world. Some scholars may not prefer to make this comparison, but there is ample evidence to suggest that both Old Testament Judaism and North American First Nations have similar structural histories. Knowing this ought to encourage more appreciation for the traditional ways of the Indigenous Peoples of North America on the part of Christians at least, but this will not likely be the case. Like their forebears, the first European invaders to this continent, many Christians may prefer to continue operating according to the uncomplicated agenda of making over the Indian people without even bothering to decipher cultural or spiritual parallels or similarities.

## A Theoretical Note

Some years ago, anthropologist Lewis H. Morgan stimulated vigorous discussion when he suggested that history is not the work of humankind, but rather a process of which man is the subject. To Morgan (1963), a thoroughgoing evolutionist, the events of human progress embody themselves, independently of the efforts of humankind, in a material record which is crystallized in institutions, usages and customs. Members of any given tribal culture inevitably proceed up the ladder of "civilization," totally unaware of the "social travail" which is the substance of human history (Terray, 1972: 16). Morgan (1963: ii) speculated that in the past

> ... savages, advancing by slow, almost imperceptible steps, attained the higher condition of barbarians; how barbarians, by similar progressive

advancement, finally attained civilization . .

Morgan elaborated on the history of several case studies of civilizations in substantiating his theory of "natural process," that is, Iroquois, Greeks, Aztecs and Roman, but otherwise left it to historians to speculate on the beginnings of inventions or institutions, and on the precise circumstances in which they made their appearance. He also postulated that the different steps in human evolution occurred most ideally in communities that were geographically isolated.

Morgan's theories notwithstanding, it is true that human societies change over time, inevitably affected by a variety of factors such as intercultural relations. The nature and pace of such change is quite unique to a given cultural configuration, and any generalizations about underlying models remain largely speculative. Certainly in comparing the development of history among the tribes of Israel with that of the North American Indigenous Peoples, no useful paradigm emerges. All that can safely be said is that at one time both civilizations manifested similar characteristics in their habits and lifestyle. As Gomme (1980: 2) notes, in every civilization there are indications that remnants of tribal life remain. People too often believe that there is no link between ancient habits and modern practices, and they do so simply on the assumption that because literature provides no direct evidence of this, there must be none. What might be even more disturbing is the possibility that many of us have not departed too much from the ways of our ancestors.

## The Hebrew Tribes

According to the biblical record, it all began with Abram of the Chaldees whom God called out of his country with the promise, "I will make you a great nation and I will bless you" (Genesis 12:2). Abram, who later became Abraham, accordingly obeyed, and his roster of successors includes his son, Isaac, and his grandson, Jacob (also called Israel), whose twelve sons became heads of the twelve tribes of Israel. Their descendants were primarily sheepherders and hunters and gatherers until they entered Egypt in a time of severe famine. The lure to relocate came from Joseph, Jacob's son, who had been sold into slavery in Egypt by his own brothers. Proving himself trustworthy, he became the right-hand man of King Pharaoh and responsible for the resettlement of Jacob's people in Egypt. Jacob's family initially consisted of sixty-six souls (Genesis 46:26), but within a century or so grew so large that their presence became a threat to the Egyptians who forced them into slavery. Moses eventually freed the children of Israel from Pharaoh's rule (dramatically portrayed in a film called "The Ten Commandments" starring Hollywood's Charleton Heston), and their further tribal wanderings lasted nearly forty years. The first five books of Moses, that is, Genesis, Exodus, Leviticus, Numbers and Deuteronomy, comprise the primary source of information regarding Israel's tribal lifestyle.

Although the terms "Israelite" and "Jew" are often used synonymously, Dana (1951: 66) argues that the latter term was primarily introduced after the post-exilic period. In 606 B.C., Nebuchadnezzar's forces removed the people of Israel to Babylon where they remained in exile for approximately seventy years. During that time, the Israelites' sense of nationalism and a desire to return to their homeland intensified. The term, "Jew" is properly a creation of the Exile, and appears in history at the time of the Restoration, seventy years later. Perhaps the change in terminology is particularly significant in light of the fact that the descendants of Israel who came out of the Babylonian Captivity had a new devotion to their moral law and to the traditions of their forefathers. They possessed a keen desire to rebuild their city and remain culturally pure by denouncing idolatry and all things Gentile. They were far more intense and exclusive in their racial loyalty than their ancestors had been in the pre-exilic period. The Babylonian captivity, therefore, was the turning point in the development of Jewish political, economic and religious exclusivity.

In the pre exilic period Old Testament Judaism, like the North American Indian Nations, could best be described as a tribal society, readily identifiable as a rural group with a distinct name and a well-defined geographic territory for which they assumed claim and responsibility. They also delineated sharply between members and non-members (Ahmed and Hart, 1984:1). This is evident in the incident when the Gibeonites entered the camp of the Israelites and tried to make a treaty with them. Having heard of the prowess of Joshua's forces in successful wars, the Gibeonites pretended to represent a faraway nation in quest of a peace treaty with Israel. When it was later discovered that their camp was only a short distance away, as punishment for their deceit Joshua relegated them permanently to the status of woodcutters and water carriers for the rest of their lives (Joshua 9:21).

Anthropologists define tribal societies as social groups that may comprise a number of sibs, bands or villages or other subgroups and which are normally in possession of a definite territory, a distinct dialect, a homogeneous and distinctive culture and have some sense of common peoplehood. This definition adequately depicts the Old Testament Tribe of Israel who descended from the loins of their father, Abraham, who settled them on their chosen land. When harsh economic conditions befell them, they migrated to Egypt where they were eventually reduced to slavery. They left Egypt under the leadership of Moses and Aaron who, with supportive Divine intervention, successfully argued their case before Pharaoh. After some forty years of wilderness wandering they reached their promised land, claimed the territory and eagerly forced out the residents. As their culture developed they gradually approached the status of statehood and appointed their first king, Saul. He was succeeded by King David, King Solomon and other successors. Eventually the Kingdom suffered a division when one of the twelve bands, the Tribe of Judah, broke away and became a separate unit. By the time the happenings in the New

Testament occurred, Israel had been transformed into a state with characteristics much resembling that of neighboring nations.

Several influences affected the development of the modern Jewish nation, one of them being Babylon. Israel was quite familiar with the ways of Babylon from ancient times, and particularly so during the time of the captivity, beginning in 606 B.C. when many Jews were taken from their homeland to Babylon. Babylonian influence is convincingly attested to by the fact that many Jewish names at that time had distinct Mesopotamian origin. Babylon influence was also evident in the area of economics, philosophy and astrology, although distinct theological influences are hard to decipher (Dana, 1951: 19).

Another influence affecting Jewish national development was Persia, particularly with regard to spiritual conceptualizations in the area of eschatology, that is, the notions of heaven and hell, the resurrection and triumph of righteousness and the forces and functions of the spirit world. Dana (1951: 20) suggests that apocalyptic interest and expression appear far more prominent in Judaism after the Persian period, and, in fact, the notion of heaven as "paradise," the concept of demonology, and the word "Satan" are of Persian origin. Jewish absorption of these concepts was probably gradual and unconscious and eventually became part of Jewish nomenclature and thought.

The world in which Christianity originated was ultimately oriental, but particularly and immediately Jewish. Jesus Christ was born a Jew, but He grew up in a culture derived from many streams of diffusion and overruled by Rome. A number of sects and political parties were in place at the time of Christ giving ample indication of a complex and perhaps overstructured society (Friesen and Boberg, 1990: 70f). The Pharisees originated as a group with the goal of fulfilling the ceremonial law, and they sought hard to live up to the letter of the law. They were a separatist people and gave Jesus a hard time when he made declarations about the Sabbath being made for man and not the other way around. Their counterparts to some extent, the Sadducees, were basically an aristocratic party, and while they agreed with the Pharisees to some extent on the importance of legalism, they rejected the doctrine of immortality and the existence of angels and spirits. The Essenes operated an isolated aesthetic community located in the desert region of the Dead Sea, and held a political position to the right of the Pharisees.

On the other end of the religious-political spectrum were the Zealots who augured for the independence of Israel from Roman rule. One group of Zealots was involved in the last fight against Roman takeover in 73 A.D. when, under the leadership of Eliezer, Son of Yair, they took to the Mountain of Metsada and held that fortress during nearly three years of seige. Eventually, Roman soldiers built a long ramp to the top of the mountain, and forced a group of Jewish slaves to push a huge wagon before them. The Zealots saw them coming and built a huge wall at the top of the mountain; unfortunately the wall was constructed of flammable material and the Romans sent flaming spears into it so it burned to the ground. The next day it was all over, the Zealots having taken their own lives. In his book, *War of the Jews,* the Jewish historian, Josephus described the heroic end of the Metsada community:

> They then chose ten men by lot out of them, to slay all the rest, everyone of whom lay himself down by his wife and children on the ground, and threw his arms around them, and they offered their necks to the stroke of those who by lot executed that melancholy office; and when these ten had, without fear, slain all before them, they made the same rule of casting lots for themselves, that he whose lot it was should first kill the other nine, and after all should kill himself. . . . The dead were about nine hundred and sixty-nine . . . The Romans could not help but wonder at the courage of their resolution. . . . (Vilnay, 1979: 322f)

The Metsada story was authenticated by an elderly Zealot women who refused to be part of the killing plan and hid herself from her comrades. It might be argued that this was a particularly horrific arrangement, but the self-styled martyrs probably reasoned that their plight at the hands of the Romans might have been even more torturous. In any event, with this approach the enemy had no reason to gloat which must have frustrated the Romans somewhat.

Like the Zealots, another group that functioned mainly according to political ambitions were the Herodians. The main thrust of this movement was to eliminate Roman domination and gain independence for Israel. Founded by Herod the Great, the group had as its major principle the idea that it was right to pay homage to a sovereign (like the Roman Emporer) who might be able to bring the friendship of Rome and other advantages, but who had no right to title to reign either by law or by religion. On this point they disagreed with the Pharisees who wanted no compromis. They basically despised Roman rule and saw no need for it. They also had no respect for a reform group that was active at this time known as the Zadokites. Their objective was to shake up the foundations of Judaistic thought and practice and modernize it. Inadvertently, by their actions they helped prepare the way for the origins of Christianity by raising crucial and relevant questions about orthodoxy.

As they gradually left their tribal ways, the Old Testament Jews placed great stress on learning, and earned themselves the title of "People of the Book." A much-quoted passage substantiates this: "Train a child in the way he should go, and when he is old he will not turn from it" (Prov. 22:6). Further, the responsibility to educate was compulsory and comprehensive.

> Hear, O Israel: The Lord our God, the Lord is one. Love the Lord your God with all your heart and with all your soul and with all your strength. These commandments that I give you today are to be upon your hearts. Impress them on your children. Talk about them when you sit at home and when you walk along the road, when you lie down and when you get up. Tie them as symbols on your hands and bind them on your foreheads. Write them on the

doorframes of your houses and on your gates. (Deut. 6:4-9)

Primarily it was considered the responsibility of the home to educate children in the sacred laws and unwritten customs. Instruction was aimed chiefly at boys who, at the age of five learned things from the Scriptures – first the Book of Leviticus and then the Pentateuch. Later the Mishnah was mastered. It consisted of the first part of the Talmud, including traditional oral interpretations of scriptural ordinances, compiled by the rabbinical scholars. Still later, the study of the rest of the Talmud would be undertaken, and if a rabbinical career was desired the student would attend an academy.

The culminating forces of Babylon, Greece and Persia converged in the first century to assist in the origin of Christianity with the birth of Jesus Christ. Rome was successful in bringing the world to a state of peace and order and in providing the facilities of communication which would foster the spreading of good news. Greece, having subdued and amalgamated the best elements of the Orient, was preparing a mind which could penetrate and interpret the profound truths of Christianity, a spirit which would furnish susceptible and fertile soil for the seed of gospel propaganda, and a language which could express the message of redemption with a beauty and accuracy which has not been equalled anywhere else in human civilization. Then, in Bethlehem, a Jewish maiden who was in that location under the requirements of Roman law, gave birth to a son whose destiny it was forever to transform the face of world religion.

The philosophical underpinnings of Christianity clearly find their taproot in the tribal configuration of ancient Israel. The Jewish oral tradition conveyed valued moral and religious beliefs to succeeding generations, and frequent exhortations by respected prophets underscored the severity of any form of deviance. When the written record appeared, the oral tradition was suddenly relegated to inferior status and the written word became law. The law then became the means by which to judge and prescribe future behaviors, undermining forever such notions as that uttered by Abraham's chief servant when he successfully reached the destination to which he was sent to fetch a bride for Abraham's son, Isaac: "I being in the way, the Lord led me to the house of my master's brethren" (Genesis 24:27 KJV)." Sadly, the warning uttered by Saint Paul years later, had already reached its fulfilment: ". . . the letter kills, but the spirit gives life" (II Corinthians 3:6b).

In tracing the evolution of Christianity from Old Testament (OT) to New Testament (NT) times it is quite illuminating to scrutinize carefully the basics of Jewish tribal spirituality and compare it with the essence of Jesus' teaching when He was asked to identify the greatest commandment:

> Jesus replied: "Love the Lord your God with all your heart and with all your soul and with all your mind. This is the first and greatest commandment. And the second is like it: Love your neighbor as yourself. All the Law and

the Prophets hang on these two commandments. (Matthew 22:37-40)

It is possible to make a case that among the tribes of Israel the sense
spirituality was gradually replaced by a more formalized set of ___
beliefs and more stringent precepts by which to live. As Knudtson and Suzuki
(1992: 13) note, traditional Nativist forms of knowledge about the natural
world, for example,

> tend to view all – or at least vast regions – of nature, often including the
> earth itself, as inherently holy rather than profane, savage, wild or waste-
> land. The landscape itself, or certain regions of it, is seen as sacred and quiv-
> ering with life. It is inscribed with meaning regarding the origins and unity
> of all life, rather than seen as mere property to be partitioned legally into
> commercial estate holdings.

Examples of this perspective are recorded in the Old Testament, e.g.,

> The earth is the Lord's, and everything in it, the world and all who live in it
> . . . (Psalm 24:1)

> The Lord reigns, let the earth be glad; let the distant shores rejoice. . . . His
> lightning lights up the world; the earth sees and trembles. The mountains
> melt like wax before the Lord, before the Lord of all the earth. (Psalm 97:1,
> 4-5)

> And they [the seraphs] were calling to one another: "Holy, holy, holy is the
> Lord Almighty; the whole earth is full of his glory." (Isaiah 6:3)

> . . . The mountains and hills will burst into song before you, and all the trees
> of the field will clap their hands. (Isaiah 55:12b)

The psalmist's picturesque descriptions of nature's wonders and their
close connection to the Creator parallel Knudtson and Suzuki's (1992: 13)
contention that "The Native Mind is imbued with a deep sense of reverence for
nature. It does not operate from an impulse to exercise human dominion over
it." Any notion that the earth must be subdued is relegated to the realm of the
Creator, that is, "How awesome is the Lord Most High, the great King over all
the earth! He subdued nations under us, peoples under our feet" (Psalm 47:2-
3).

It is clear that for tribal cultures the rhythms of the universe are to be
respected and held in awe. Humanity has an obligation to maintain the balance
and health of the natural world as a solemn spiritual daily duty. As the indica-
tors of a more formalized approach to social structure and governance evolve,
however, attitudes towards the earth's processes are also transformed. When
the tribes of Israel were first called into existence under the leadership of
Moses, they were probably bound by kinship lines. Gradually, a sense of peoplehood developed and they began to envisage having dominion over a section
of promised land. During their wilderness wanderings their territorial basis
was not precisely defined. Schapera (1967: 219f) suggests that as tribal societies gain access to permanent territory and develop a degree of institutional

stability, the community tends to become more heterogeneous and the functions of government become more numerous and varied.

## Development of the Jewish State

For many generations the tribes of Israel were faithfully served by elders commonly known as judges or prophets. One of the better known elders was Samuel, son of Elkanah and Hannah, who was born in the hills of Ephraim. Before his birth he was dedicated to the office of Nazarite and as a young child he was placed in the temple where he ". . . ministered before the Lord" under the supervision of Eli the priest (I Samuel 2:18). Samuel served the tribes faithfully for many years, but as he grew older he appointed his sons as judges for the nation. It turned out that his sons did not walk in the fear of the Lord as their father had done, and the leaders of Israel decided that it was time for a change. "Now appoint a king to lead us," (I Samuel 8:5b) they told Samuel, but this request greatly displeased him.

Samuel took the matter to the Lord in prayer and Jehovah assured him,

> Listen to all that the people are saying to you; it is not you they have rejected, but they have rejected me as their king. . . . Now listen to them and warn them solemnly and let them know what the king who will reign over them will do. (I Samuel 8:7, 9)

The biblical record goes on to elucidate the demands that a king would make on the people; he would take their sons and force them to do a variety of tasks such as enlist in the military to either make weapons or fight in the army or till the king's lands. Daughters would be taken away and compelled to be perfumers, cooks or bakers. In addition, the king would confiscate fields, vineyards and olive groves and give them to his attendants. He would lay claim to a tithe of the people's income and possessions and confiscate the best of their flocks for his own.

Despite Samuel's pleadings, the people ignored his warnings. They were ready for statehood and requested a king to lead them into battle like other nations around them. They no longer wanted to be different; they wanted to fit in (I Samuel 8:20). Samuel cautioned them that if they chose to ignore Jehovah's word and went ahead with the appointment of a king, there would be no relief from God if things went awry. Soon after, Saul, the son of Kish, from the Tribe of Benjamin, was anointed king. In order to impress the people about the continued need to fear God, Samuel made a powerful speech and ordered thunder and lightning in the sky. This caused great uneasiness in the camp and the people began to fear they had made a mistake in demanding the appointment of a king. Samuel assured them that if they continued to worship Jehovah, even with a king, conditions would assume some semblance of normalcy.

King Saul began his reign by selecting three thousand men and attacking the Philistines at Geba. The custom was that an elder would offer a burnt offering to Jehovah before the attack began, which meant waiting for Samuel to do so, but Saul was impatient, and presided at the ceremony himself. When Samuel arrived he reprimanded Saul for his impatience, but Saul insisted that the prophet had been late and the enemy was prepared to attack. In his defence, Saul stated:

> When I saw that the men were scattering, and that you did not come at the set time, and that the Philistines were assembling at Mishna,. . . I felt compelled to offer the burnt offering. (I Samuel 13:11b-12)

Some time later, Saul prepared his army to attack another enemy, the Amalakites. His ambush of the enemy was successful, and Saul was tempted by the spoils the enemy left behind when they fled. He had been warned by Samuel that nothing was to be taken in the raid, since this would displease the Lord, but Saul could not contain himself. Tempted by the rich bounty that would be his, he had his men save some herds of cattle and sheep as a reward for his efforts. When Samuel arrived on the scene he enquired of Saul as to the noise of cattle and sheep he was hearing. Saul put the blame on his soldiers, claiming that they had spared the best of the sheep and cattle in order to sacrifice them to the Lord. Samuel knew Saul was lying and called him on it. He demanded:

> Does the Lord delight in burnt offerings and sacrifices as much as in obeying the voice of the Lord? To obey is better than sacrifice, and to heed is better than the fat of the rams. For rebellion is like the sin of divination, and arrogance like the evil of idolatry. Because you have rejected the word of the Lord, he has rejected you as king. (I Samuel 15:22-23)

So it seemed that everything that Samuel had warned the people about in terms of obtaining a king was coming true. For Saul, unfortunately, after this disobedient act, everything was downhill. Unbeknownst to Saul, Samuel went about anointing a shepherd boy, David, as the next king. When Saul eventually found out he grew jealous of David and sought to kill him. In the meantime David endeared himself to the people by his music, bravery and military skill in slaying the giant, Goliath, but this did not deter Saul from trying to carry out his mission. Saul's own son, Jonathan, was a close friend to David and even tried to protect David from Saul's anger. At one point, David had opportunity to kill Saul, but he refused to do so on grounds that he would not slay the Lord's anointed (I Sam 24:10).

In the downward spiral of his own spirituality, King Saul eventually sought out the "Witch of Endor" to enquire about his future. He disguised himself at the encounter, and requested that the woman bring up the spirit of Samuel, now deceased, with whom he could consult. The woman did so, but when she saw the face of Samuel, she knew who Saul was and cried out, "Why have you deceived me? You are Saul" (I Samuel 28:12b). Saul assured her that no harm would come to her, but the message he received from the old prophet's spirit was less than satisfactory. Beginning with an expression of irritation that Saul had disturbed his spirit, Samuel reminded Saul that the Lord had turned his back on him and as punishment would allow the Nation of Israel to fall into the hands of the Philistines. Shortly thereafter, Saul took his own life by throwing himself off his horse and deliberately falling on his own sword (I Samuel 31:4).

As Israel continued to develop as a nation state, their next king, David, continued to clear out the promised land and claim it for his people. At one point he declared his intent to build a great temple of worship to God, another indication of rising statehood. King David was discouraged from doing so by the Almighty on the basis that he was a man of war, and, therefore, David was informed, his son, Solomon would built the temple. Like his predecessor, Saul, David also fulfilled some of Samuel's negative forcastings about the inconvenience of having kings, but in the end he remained in God's good books. David's successors were often judged by whether or not they "walked in all the ways of David [their] father" (II Kings 22:2).

By the time Solomon arrived on the throne, Israel had sufficient experience with statehood that they knew what they wanted of their monarch. Equal to the challenge, Solomon requested that Jehovah reward his faith with extra wisdom so he could serve his people better. He immediately set himself to building the temple envisaged by his father, David, and embarked on a series of interstate liaisons both to obtain necessary materials and to further trade. The installation of the sacred Ark of the Covenant in the temple marked the formalization of the temple as a permanent worship site for the nation. The Ark of the Covenant was significant because it was viewed as a holy thing, and represented the presence of God. Priests carried it for the tribe as they left Egypt and throughout their wilderness sojourn. The costs of Solomon's elaborate temple constructions and resultant tax burden on the people caused a certain national restlessness, however, and Solomon soon found himself dealing with the root of insurrection (I Kings 11:26f). Israel as a nation had come of age.

One of the rebels who opposed Solomon was Jeroboam, whom Solomon had elevated to the position of superintendent of taxation and labor over the Tribe of Ephraim. Jeroboam's revolt was so successful that he eventually became king of the northern Tribes of Israel shortly after Solomon's son, Rehoboam, took office as king. Rehoboam refused to take the advice of his counsellors to reduce the tax burden inflicted by his father, and there was open rebellion among the tribes. Rehoboam was forced to flee and his kingdom was reduced to include only the Tribes of Judah and Benjamin. Still, during Rehoboam's reign a degree of peace was restored although the kingdom was never again reunited. Within five years of his ascension to the throne, Rehoboam's kingdom was invaded by an army from Egypt and the capital City of Jerusalem was taken. Rehoboam made peace with the invaders by supplying them with all of the treasures of the temple.

Jeroboam, in the meantime, denounced the God of Israel and discouraged the annual pilgrimage to Jerusalem. Instead he established shrines at Dan and Bethel, sanctuaries of venerable antiquity located at the extremities of the kingdom. He disregarded prophecies that he would be replaced by a king, Josiah, who would dismantle Rehoboam's sacrilegious altars and reestablish the worship of Jehovah, the God of Israel. When Rehoboam's son, Rehoboam II, took over from his father he presided over a very prosperous kingdom and freed Israel from the terror of Syria, their neighboring enemy. Religiously he maintained the same perspective as his father, ignoring the prophecies of Daniel the prophet, and Amos the sheepherder, who warned of God's wrath (Amos 2:6f, 8:2). Eventually, Amos' warnings became reality, and by the time of the birth of Jesus Christ Israel was only a tiny island in the sea of the mighty Roman Empire.

## The Rise of Christianity

The first historic mention of the Roman Empire in the Bible is recorded in I Maccabeus 1:10, about the year, 161 B.C. In 65 B.C., when Syria was made a Roman province by Pompey, the Jews were still governed by one of the Asmonean princes. The next year Pompey himself marched an army into Judea and took Jerusalem. In 30 B.C. Herod the Great was made king by Antony's interest and confirmed in the kingdom by Augustus. Israel now became a tributary of Rome and Judea a mere appendage of the province of Syria governed by a procurator who resided at Caesarea. At the time when Israel was submerged by Rome the empire was basically confined to a narrow strip encircling the Mediterranean Sea. Pompey soon added Asia Minor and Syria, and Caesar added Gaul; thus the building continued. Eventually the kingdom stretched from the Atlantic in the west; and the Euphrates in the east; to the deserts of Africa, the cataracts of the Nile and the Arabian deserts in the south; and the British Channel, the Rhine, the Danube and the Black Sea in the north.

The condition of the Roman Empire at the time when Christianity appeared was amply represented in the words of Saint Paul in the phrase, "The fullness of time was come" (Galatians. 4:4 KJV). The general peace within the limits of the empire, the formation of military roads, the suppression of piracy, the march of the legions, the voyages of the corn fleets, the general increase of traffic, the spread of the Latin language in the west as Greek had already spread in the east, the external unity of the empire, offered facilities hitherto unknown for the spread of the worldwide religion. Roman leaders had the philosophy of reducing all its subjects to an even level and therefore tried to break down the pride of privileged races and national religions. In a sense the empire seemed bent on fulfilling the intent of the biblical premise, God "hath made of one blood all nations of men for to dwell on the face of the earth . . ." (Acts 17:26 KJV).

Perhaps the most striking feature of the Roman empire was its fermenting, deep and widespread corruption which seemed to defy any human remedy. The stark contrast of the high moral lifestyle preached by John the Baptist and Jesus Christ lured many to the new philosophy. The Gospel experienced its greatest expansion when Saul of Tarsus (later to become Paul), was converted and undertook a series of missionary journeys to surrounding areas such as Achaia, Asia, and Macedonia. Many of the epistles in the New Testament were penned to congregations founded by Paul's ministry, that is, at Corinth, Galatia, Ephesus, Philippi, Colosse and Thessalonica. By 135 A.D., however, Jerusalem was made a heathen city and the name of Judea was changed to Syria Palestina. Jews were forbidden to set foot in Jerusalem and Palestine basically had no history for many years until it fell into the hands of the Turks. During the 11th and 12th centuries it was made the scene of crusades and held by the Turks until 1917 when it was liberated and passed under the British Protectorate. The State of Israel was reinstated on May 14, 1948 and, with the exception of continuing Israeli-Arab tensions, has flourished.

## Modern Israel

After being scattered throughout various countries for many generations and suffering persecution at the hands of many nations, the tenacious Jews have at long last retrieved their homeland in Israel. Most recent conquests against them were waged by Germany under the rule of Adolph Hitler and by Communists in Russia. In 1945, the Anglo-American Commission conducted an inquiry and agreed with a 1937 report which recommended the partition of Palestine into two sovereign states. The residents of Palestine, including Jews, Arabs and other groups, rejected the proposal and subsequent ones, and on May 15, 1948, it was announced that British forces then occupying Palestine would be withdrawn. The independent State of Israel was immediately declared and honored by both the United States and Russia. Since then the new nation has fought offensively and defensively in wars to protect infringement on Jewish lands. Of her ability to wage war it has been said that Israel fights in "a unique way, one that combined biblical inspiration and patriotism with the intellectual sophistication of the strategy of indirection" (Schweitzer, 1971: 294).

In 1967 Israel was involved in the Six Day War that ended with the tiny country of nearly four million people stretching to the size of 43 000 acres of land. The successful results of that war also yielded the victorious nation with control over nearly one million Arabs who previously occupied the accumulated lands. Jerusalem became the capital of the new country as it was during the four hundred year period from the Kings of Israel and Judah, from David and Solomon to Jehoiachin and Zedekiah. It is also the historic home of the prophets, Ezekiel, Habakkuk, Haggai, Isaiah, Jeremiah, Micah and Zechariah.

In Israel, ancient tribal enemies, Arab and Jew, live side by side although not always peaceably. The country is frequently in the news as the sons of Israel, descendants of Ishmael and Isaac, lay claim to their father's blessing. Jewish and Arabic schools, hostels and businesses are often located side by side, but the clientele is selective. Only the untrained eye of the casual tourist will bypass the sharply divided yet invisible lines that pock the country. Such is the destiny of a tribal culture turned state.

# Four

# First Nations and Hebrew Tribal Societies:
# Contrasts and Comparisons

The latest investigations respecting the early condition of the human race, are tending to the conclusion that mankind commenced their career at the bottom of the scale and worked their way up from savagery to civilization through the slow accumulations of experimental knowledge.

– stated in 1877 by Lewis H. Morgan (1963: 3)

A century ago, many anthropologists still promulgated the ancient notion that societal progress was intricately connected to technology. As Morgan's statement attests, it was widely believed that the progressive development of inventions, discoveries and institutions supported the notion that since the origin of people, their aggressive efforts had helped them to ascend to a higher rung on the ladder of evolutionary civilization. This perspective was premised on the European-inherited notion that the tribal societies encountered by the first visitors to North America were vastly inferior to those they had left behind in Spain, France or England. Morgan cited seven proofs of the latter's success including more finely developed forms of subsistence, government, speech, family, religion and architecture, and the origin of the notion of property ownership.

Morgan insisted that the Aryan kinship family enjoyed "intrinsic superiority" when compared with the First Peoples of North America. His concocted scale revealed mental and moral inferiority on the part of the Indigenous Peoples due to cultural underdevelopment and inexperience and hindered by animal appetites and passions. Small wonder that the Aboriginal tribal configurations encountered by the first Europeans in North American were immediately denigrated and still continue to be unappreciated. As a corollary note on Morgan's analysis, he did admit that the vast "improvements" of modern society, particularly the quest for property ownership, had produced unmanageable power quests that would surely be the unmaking of civilization. He projected that the attainment of the highest plane of civilization that could be envisaged might even imply a return to ancient ways that respected liberty, equality and fraternity. This future state was not to be confused with savage or barbaric communalism, because tribal configurations could at best hold such ideals in embryonic form (Dippie, 1985: 110).

The emergence of Morgan's ideal state may yet become reality. The need to respect the earth and all living things once so clearly exhibited by tribal societies is today being hailed as an urgent need. John Collier, Indian Commissioner for the United States, once commented on the traditional Indian reverence for the earth, "They [the First Nations] had what the world has lost. They have it now. What the world has lost the world must have again, lest it die" (Bordewich, 1996: 71). Knudtson and Suzuki (1992) are optimistic in observing that increasing numbers of people are beginning to recognize that the degree of respect for the earth held by many ancient societies must be regained – and soon. They maintain that

> If biodiversity and ecosystem integrity are critical to salvaging some of the skin of life on earth, then every successful fight to protect the land of Indigenous Peoples is a victory for all humanity and for all living things. (Knudtson and Suzuki, 1992: xxxiv)

They go on to argue that the ecological impact of industrial civilization and the sheer weight of human numbers is now global and is changing the biosphere with frightening speed. It is clear that such problems as global warming, species depletion, ozone depletion and pollution cannot be resolved by any band-aid approach such as higher taxes, government intervention or recycling. A radical approach that consists of new ways of relating to the universe is both urgent and necessary. Perhaps the power and relevance of ancient tribal knowledge and world-view may be called upon to lend a hand.

There is a prophecy among the Lakota that in the future people of other races and cultures will come to the First Nations seeking the wisdom of the people. They will realize that they are out of balance with the universe and out of right relation with the Great Mystery and Grandmother earth despite their many packed houses of worship. Future generations of Indians must therefore be prepared to help them when they come. It will be a time of renewal (Kaltreider, 1998: 91).

## Tribal Configurations

## Aboriginal Origins

Scientists always seem to have an explanation for the unknown, usually in the form of an unsupported theory without which nothing apparently seems to make sense. This is certainly true with regard to the history of North American First Nations whose ancestors are labelled Paleo Indians or Clovis People by anthropologists. About the best explanation of their lifestyle that can be rendered is that conjecture tells us that they were big-game hunters and gatherers, but

We know nothing about the clothing, shelters, or social organization of the peoples who constituted this tradition and very little about their appearance, values, and religious orientation. (Bowden, 1981: 3)

This admission has not hindered the speculative process, which, in fairness, is not entirely without evidence. Several excavated archeological sites have verified the theory about the existence of big game. A recent dig at Big Springs, South Dakota, for example, has verified the previous existence of several species of mammals whose perfectly-preserved remains were discovered in a sink-hole where these creatures perished when they came to drink. The bones of one species of mammals found in the sink-hole show them to have measured nearly five metres (over fourteen feet) in height.

It is becoming evident that Aboriginal Peoples of the various culture areas in North America lived full and probably satisfying lives, beginning with the fact that food was plentiful. At the time of contact, there were thriving agricultural communities around the Great Lakes Region, in the Eastern Woodlands, in the southwest and as far north as North Dakota. Fishing was a major source of food supply on both east and west coasts as well as among the Plateau Indians in what is now the British Columbia Interior. When the Woodland Peoples migrated to the plains several centuries ago they developed a nomadic lifestyle following the migration patterns of the buffalo. The base of all of these cultures rested on a philosophy of ready adjustment to changes necessitated by natural forces. Many of the more sedentary civilizations left impressive remains behind which gave a clear indication of the extent of their technological genius. The eastern moundbuilders bequeathed thousands of huge temple mounds as well as burial and effigy mounds, some of which had lunar alignments. The Anasazi of the southwest left huge walled cities, some of them five stories high. Their neighbors, the Hohokam, dug hundreds of miles of water-carrying canals, many of which are still in use today. Only the Plains tribes left little physical evidence of the magnitude and genius of their cultures save for buffalo jumps and remains of winter camps and other sites of interest to archeologists.

## Tribal World View

It is useful to researchers to note that Aboriginal societies today much more resemble the lifestyles of their forebears than do those social systems that were imported from Europe. The genius of this reality is that it is still possible to study and comprehend the workings of many Native societies in that they reflect the essence of many traditional ways. In addition, the cultural revitalization movement that is active among Indigenous Peoples today has placed new emphasis on old ways so that elders are being sought out to explain the old ways and bring them back into practice. Many ancient customs and rituals that were once deemed lost are being reenacted with new meaning as elders begin to share their knowledge. Fortunately, these have not been stamped out, for many of them were simply taken underground and held there until the time was right to release them. Illustrative of the rebirth of Aboriginal ceremonies include the sundance, potlatch, pipe ceremonies, use of sweetgrass, transfer ceremonies and a host of other rituals (Lincoln, 1985).

Lewis Morgan and his colleagues made the unfortunate ethnocentric error of assuming that cultural development always implies improvement. They also assumed that the Euro-American model of cultural development could well serve as an international, indeed global model of human achievement, and should be copied by civilizations everywhere. A reexamination of this rather haughty perspective has convinced even anthropologists that they may have been too hasty in denouncing Aboriginal tribal cultures as inferior.

The social and spiritual aspects of pre-contact Indian tribal societies constitute the most parallel points of comparison with the Tribe of Israel. Seven such points of comparison may be made, although the discussion will primarily deal with the Canadian Plains' Indian milieu, which is best known to the author. Despite this delimitation, however, there is reason to believe that Aboriginal peoples from many different areas of this continent traditionally ascribed to a similar metaphysical perspective while it remained unaffected by immigration, industry or imported forms of technology. It is necessary, of course, to acknowledge the diversity that existed among traditional Indian cultures with respect to their means of obtaining food, cultural practices, lifestyle, and so on, but the basic theological system to which they all subscribed was fundamentally tribal. The intent of this discussion is to explain that world view for the purpose of showing its remarkable similarity to the Old Testament Hebrew Weltanschauung.

The need for this book stems from the fact that while the Weltanschauung of the First Peoples is markedly different from that of Euro-Americans, it does bear a striking resemblance to that of Old Testament Israel. This is significant to note since the western world, as influenced by Christianity, places a high value on Jewish cultural development and achievement while neglecting that of the Aboriginal Peoples. The purpose here is to illustrate that the two have remarkably similar histories, social structures and spiritual repertoires.

The approach taken to delineating the identified philosophical similarities is through an examination of traditional core values which are still well-preserved among many Native tribes.

## 1. A Holistic Perspective

... the earth shall be full of the knowledge of the Lord ... (Isaiah 11:9b KJV)

It is hard for non-Aboriginals to comprehend the implications of a holistic view of the universe, but Indians have always believed that all phenomena, including both material and non-material elements, are connected and inter-connected. The interconnectedness of all things of earth means that everything we do has consequences that reverberate through the system of which we are a part (Suzuki, 1997: 102). Native people do not adhere to any "scientific" breakdown of how people function or how the universe operates. The non-Native scientific view further allows and encourages the development of sep-arate "hard-core" academic disciplines which seek to identify and explain the various components of cosmic and material phenomena, such as biophysics, astrochemistry, biotechnology, nuclear mathematics, social physiology, and so on. Although the proponents of each of these areas of expertise will make sophisticated claims about interdisciplinary parallels and concerns, there is always an element of professional ethnocentrism involved in their scientific deliberations.

This delineation of disciplinary specialties is quite foreign to the First Nations' way of thinking. Aboriginal People view the world as an intercon-nected series of only sometimes distinguishable or comprehensible elements. They experience no uneasiness at the thought of multiple realities simultane-ously operant in the universe, and they do not differentiate among the varieties or qualities of entities, that is between material or non-material elements. Their world view allows for the possibility that a variety of "structurally-different" elements may simultaneously be active in the process of holistic healing. This also explains why dreams and visions comprise as welcome a source of knowl-edge as scientifically-derived truths or personal experience. In short, you never know where you might gain knowledge or where you might learn something.

It is truly doubtful that a two-tiered universe of spirit and mass can be con-structed on the basis of Old Testament theology since the Tribe of Israel saw the hand of God in everything they did. They perceived the universe as a unity. Jehovah supplied the people with food, sometimes providing it in quite mirac-ulous ways such as the great flock of quail (Exodus 16:13), or in the form of bread from heaven shaped like little white flakes (Exodus 16:14). The produce of the earth was always perceived as beautiful and glorious and a gift from God (Isaiah 4:2). Jehovah helped the nation in times of war, although some-times not in an entirely impartial manner, for example, in their battle against the Amalakites (Exodus 17:11-13). Moses, who was watching the battle go on, discovered that as long as he raised his hands towards heaven, the Israelite army was in a winning position. Whenever he lowered his hands, the Amalakites began to conquer. When his arms grew tired he put them on a stone, one on each side, aided by his brother, Aaron, and a colleague named Hur. Thus the Israelites were victorious.

When the Hebrews finally reached their promised land, after nearly forty years of wilderness wandering, the Israelites found it necessary to drive out a host of other tribes who had long been resident in that location – Amorites, Canaanites, Hivites, Jebuzites, Midianities, Perizzites, Philistines, and so on (Joshua 9:1-2). Their successes in battle were attributed to their finding favor with Jehovah who had earlier promised the territory to their father, Abraham.

The psalmist often appears to burst into song when he extols the virtues of the earth as gifts to God's people. The "whole earth" appears to be benefactor of this generosity: "Sing to the Lord a new song," he says, "sing to the Lord all the earth" (Psalm 96:1). "The Lord reigns, let the earth be glad" (Psalm 97:1). Further, ". . . all the ends of the earth have seen the salvation of our God" (Psalm 98:3c). Undoubtedly, the perspective of a unity of living things and the interconnectedness of all earthly phenomena was common to both Aboriginal and Jewish tribal societies.

Indian tribal appreciation for the spiritual dimension has been underestimated and misunderstood by researchers from the time of first contact. Not recognizing the nature of Indian spirituality, since the Europeans had left their own tribal origins far behind, the newcomers underestimated the extent to which spiritual concerns were valued by Native peoples as a significant part of daily life. In fact, the invaders assumed that the Indians were not even spiritually-oriented in the conventional sense. At most the Indigenous People were accused of worshipping "evil spirits." European thinkers tended to place great importance on institutionalized religion which was best delineated in terms of elaborately-decorated physical structures and strictured procedures when contrasted with the Aboriginal format, and from their perspective there were hardly any points by which meaningfully to compare the two systems. In an interesting twist, the clash of the two traditions produced a regrettable functionality of sorts. European spokespersons, particularly those backed by a religious hierarchy, believed in making authoritative claims about the various workings of the universe. Indians, on the other hand, were a listening people; if anyone did make such a claim, he or she was certainly given an audience because not to do so might be to risk losing valuable insights. After all, no one would knowingly make a false claim about having a particular spiritual insight because the fear of being exposed was strong. One's claims to truth were expected to be validated through subsequent happenings. After contact the arrangement was that the claim-making invaders gained a dominant position in negotiations based on their particular interpretation of who was in possession of a superior theological system.

The Native tribal orientation towards the universe naturally blossomed into a resignation to work with forces of the universe. The power of these forces was obvious, yet rhythmic, and by respecting these reliable patterns, it was possible to sustain a form of cultural life on earth. A further extension of this mind-set was an inherent warning not to seek to dominate or exploit nature, but to work in harmony with it. During their wilderness wanderings the

Tribe of Israel was also subject to natural forces. Thanks to the leadership of Moses, however, they overcame some of the conditions that appeared to be stacked against them.

Tribal cultures have always had a profound respect for the earth, largely because they appreciated its produce for sustenance. As Aldo Leobold has noted,

> The land is not merely soil; it is a foundation of energy flowing through a circuit of souls, plants and animals. . . . An ethic to supplement and guide the economic relation to land presupposes the existence of some mental image of land as a biotic mechanism. We can be ethical only in relation to something we can see, feel, understand, love, or otherwise have faith in. (quoted in Suzuki, 1997: 104)

The concept of personal or group ownership of land was foreign to Indian tribal societies at the time of treaty-signing. Their concept of a treaty was one of creating a good and lasting friendship between two nations who at one time were at war with one another. Therefore, when the Canadian government began the process of signing the ten written treaties in 1871 with First Nations across the country, they were building on a process that was quite familiar to the Aboriginal peoples. Most tribes had a long history of treaty-making with other nations, usually negotiated as a symbol of peace, and accompanied by the ceremonial smoking of the pipe and the exchange of gifts. To Native people, smoking the pipe was analogous to the non-Native practice of swearing on the Bible (Treaty 7, 1996: 68). Some historians also estimate that before 1871 when the formal treaty-signing process began, as many as 500 treaties had been signed between First Nations and European governments. Unlike Treaties Nos. 1-10, the previous treaties were primarily friendship treaties intended to hinder the outbreak of war. To this day many Native leaders regret having been forced to give up their lands when they signed the ten major treaties.

By contrast, when the Tribe of Israel entered their promised land they were told by the Creator not to have anything to do with treaty-making. They were to possess the land in every sense of the word and leave no enemy unconquered. The single exception came with the Gibeonites, who were resident in Palestine, and deceived the Israelite leader, Joshua, into thinking that they were from outside the country. As noted earlier, when Joshua discovered that the Gibeonites were next in line to be conquered he punished them for their deception (Joshua 9:27).

Traditionally, tribal societies relied on the oral tradition for passing along revered cultural knowledge. This was done largely through storytelling. The oral tradition afforded an entirely flexible dimension to tribal philosophy with the inbuilt possibility of reacting to unexpected changes much in the way that nature does. Contrasted with the current preoccupation for recording every-thing, an Oglala elder, Four Guns once stated:

> Many of the white man's ways are past our understanding. . . . They put a great store upon writing; there is always a paper.

> The white people must think paper has some mysterious power to help them in the world. The Indian needs no writings; words that are true sink deep into his heart, where they remain. He never forgets them. On the other hand, if the white man loses his paper, he is helpless.

> I once heard one of their preachers say that no white man was admitted to heaven unless there were writings about him in a great book! (Friesen, 1995a: 38)

Biblical scholars maintain that the written tradition was common to Old Testament Israel and, beginning with the Book of Genesis, Moses dutifully recorded the story of his tribe. The dates of events recorded in the Book of Genesis are estimated between 1491-1451 B.C. The first five books of the Bible, all allegedly written by Moses, are known as the Pentateuch and include Genesis, Exodus, Leviticus, Numbers and Deuteronomy. Genesis covers the first 2 369 years of Jewish history, Exodus records their escape from Egypt and wilderness wanderings, and Leviticus outlines the sacred rituals and cere-monies celebrated by the tribe. Numbers picks up the story of the Exodus from the time of their leaving Mount Sinai to the reaching of the promised land, and Deuteronomy contains three primary discourses delivered by Moses prior to his death. The Book of Leviticus is of primary concern in this context because the ceremonies described therein show a great deal of similarity to those prac-ticed by the First Nations of North America. Perhaps all tribal societies once developed a similar form of ritualistic practice as a result of their transportable cultures.

## 2. Earth Veneration

> It was you who set all the boundaries of the earth; you made both sum-mer and winter. (Psalm 74:17)

In the traditional world of the First Nations there was only one universal and absolute truth – the universe exists and its rhythms must be respected. Often described in terms such as respect for nature or working in harmony with nature, the underlying truth requires much more pondering. Coupled with the concept of interconnectedness, for the Indian the universe remains the object of reverence albeit veiled in mystery. There are no satisfying scientific explanations in this approach, and the deeper mysteries are only partially understood through non-scientific, spiritual truths or through mythology steeped in time.

Belief in the eternal mystique of the universe prohibits the idea of exploitation or domination. An unknowable and hallowed entity should not be approached in any other manner but with respect, awe and obeisance. One should not tamper with the elements or workings of the universe, but respect its modus operandi. As the mysterious but Divinely-controlled source of life and sustenance the earth's power is enigmatic but reliable. To question or seek to tamper with its rhythmic functions would be tantamount to playing God.

Pelletier (Frideres, 1974: 105-106), describes the difference between an Indian and non-Indian approach to the universe in a scene that places him on the top of a mountain in British Columbia. There he imagines he has been assigned the awesome responsibility of improving his natural environment. His first inclination is to stock the sky with a few more birds or perhaps move a few clouds around to provide balance. Then his eye falls on an old plank lying on the ground at his feet and he decides to relocate it to a more appropriate place. The plank is obviously hindering the grass from growing. As he lifts the plank he notices that the underside of it contains a whole colony of insect life. Ants are scrambling to move their eggs to safety, woodlice are digging to get down into the ground, earthworms are coiled up like snakes, and a spider is staring him straight in the face demanding, "What have you done to my world?" Pelletier immediately puts the board down as close to the original place as possible, and apologizes to the insects for disturbing their society. Then he gives thanks for the lesson that he is being taught not to interfere with the doings of the universe.

Tribal cultures all around the world once respected the natural workings of the earth, but once the infusion of industrialization and technology was realized, this ethic became frustrated. True, some of the inventions of the new outlook proved satisfying and convenient, but the effect on the environment was beyond comprehension. In the conquering mode of today's urban development campaign, the mandate is still to rearrange the earth in a pattern that is virtually indistinguishable when compared with the previous format; nothing will remain untouched, if not completely destroyed. This, after all, is progress. Imagine a traditionally-minded Aboriginal bystander solemnly pondering the process, wondering if "progress" will eventually run its course and Mother Earth be allowed to resume her natural course.

Soon after government negotiators completed the signing of Treaty Seven with the Blood Tribe of southern Alberta, officials suggested that the tribe consider selling off some of their land to provide revenue. This idea was greeted by one chief's unequivocal announcement, "The grass is for sale, but not the earth." Implicit in this pronouncement was the belief that the resources of Mother Earth were for everyone's benefit but the earth itself should not be divided up for personal gain nor for private ownership.

The downside of earth reverence, if it may be so labelled, is that the resultant attitude towards the universe can take many forms. The strong penchant towards "earth maintenance," so strongly valued by many successors of the

European tradition, for example, might be viewed by Native people as comprising a form of tampering with the operations of the universe. Nowhere is there a better illustration of this than when formerly-developed communities wither and fall into disuse. Abandoned townsites serve to substantiate the Indian view that non-Native people tend to build and abandon or destroy. They dig holes, erect buildings, lay paved roads and streets, and install elaborate underground wiring and pipe systems. When a town dies, however, in many cases the modern trappings of convenience are left to decay, often inflicting permanent damage to the environment as well as comprising an eyesore (even by non-Native standards). This situation Native people find quite intolerable. In their view, in time, happily the earth will return to find its own level – provided that no irreparable damage has been done in the meantime.

The First Nations of North America see themselves as part of a great chain of existence that includes all aspects of creation; all elements in this natural chain are interrelated and interdependent. If any single element is subjected to undue attention or pressure or is tampered with, there will be repercussions in the grand scheme of things. Scientists may wish to argue with this layman's view of things, because the western perspective conceives of the universe in terms of chains of cause-and-effect. Things are what they are, and do what they do, largely because antecedent things did what they did and were what they were. The underlying assumption is that if we design the right tools and approaches we will be able to understand those chains of cause-and-effect and perhaps tailor them to our own objectives. However, when one ponders the tremendous changes that have occurred in society in quite recent decades, which have affected the workings of the environment, the mind boggles. If the earth has been a working enterprise for "millions of years" as we have been led to believe by those same scientists, even a non-scientist can imagine what the effect of increased chemical use and pollution – of the earth, air and water – might be to the universe. This damage to the universe has been accomplished in only a few years, which amounts to a relatively insignificant hiccup in light of the duration of the earth's existence. It may not be true that every irregularity caused by a scientific adjustment can also be rectified by still another scientific adjustment. If this is so, surely the matter is at least cause for serious concern if not diligent study.

The Hebraic attitude towards the universe was classically tribal. The people believed there was a close correlation between the extent to which God would bless them and their regard for the elements of the universe. For example,

> When I shut up the heavens so that there was no rain, or command locusts
> to devour the land or send a plague among my people, if my people, who are
> called by my name, will humble themselves and pray and seek my face and
> turn from their wicked ways, then I will hear from heaven and will forgive
> their sin and will heal their land. (II Chronicles 7:13-14)

Divine approval, which was evident in the form of ample sustenance and good health, was dependant on the tribe's humility, prayers and repentance. In the words of Lame Deer, a Sioux Elder, "we are part of the nature around us, and the older we get the more we come to look like it. In the end we become part of the landscape with a face like the Badlands" (Lame Deer and Erdoes, 1972: 130).

## 3. Being, Not Doing

> And Jesus answered and said unto her, Martha, Martha, thou art careful and troubled about many things: But one thing is needful: and Mary hath chosen that good part which shall not be taken away from her. (Luke 10:41-42 KJV)

This passage refers to the proceedings during a visit made by Jesus to the home of his friends, Mary, Martha and Lazarus. During the visit, Martha "was distracted by all the preparations that had to be made" (Luke 10:39b), so that she missed out entirely on the conversation. She complained to Jesus that her sister, Mary, was not helping her with the business of hosting and should be reprimanded. At that point Christ admonished her about being a busybody for no particularly good reason when instead she should have been engaging in spiritual discussion. He then commended Mary for showing good judgment.

One of the hardest "truths" for adherents to the work-ethic to accept is for anyone to claim that work of itself has no virtue. Martha would probably have needed to lot of coaxing to have believed that. Yet, an important underlying presupposition of the traditional Native lifestyle was to shun work for its own sake, and even demean any colleague who intrinsically bought into the work ethic. Virtue was seen as emanating from living in the "perennial now," and staying in tune with one's spiritual destiny. Staying alive was a principal occupation of ancient tribal societies and it was accomplished via hunting and gathering, through agriculture or via a combination of these activities. For hunting societies, it was necessary to pursue game only when the larder was empty. Once it was full, due to the results of a successful hunt, it was time to celebrate.

The First Nations' attitude towards work originated in a present-oriented, survival-centred society. Game was hunted to fulfil present needs, and with the exception of being stored as pemmican, meat could not be preserved for long periods of time. When the circumstances of hunting and gathering called for hard work, it was done, but there was no concept of holding a job in order to be "doing something" or as a means of validating one's existence. Work was undertaken to fulfil a specific task or to satisfy a pressing need – nothing more.

During their nearly forty years of wilderness wanderings the Tribe of Israel operated on a similar kind of schedule. When they needed food or water, the Creator provided it, albeit sometimes through quite unusual means. While travelling through the Desert of Sin, for example, they camped for the night at

Rephidim, but the people complained about the inadequate water supply. Moses grew frustrated and cried out to the Lord, "What am I to do with these people? They are almost ready to stone me" (Exodus 17:4). Moses was then ordered by God to strike a rock and water would come out of it and thus meet the needs of the people. Moses did so in the sight of the elders of the tribe and they called the name of the place Massah and Meribah to commemorate both the people's lack of faith and God's miraculous provision.

A similar procedure by which to obtain necessary food was once practiced among the Mandan Indians of what is now North Dakota. Although primarily an agricultural people, the Mandans and their neighbors, the Arikara and Hidatsa, also hunted buffalo. Being a sedentary society, however, they did not find it convenient to engage in long distance hunting. They preferred not to wander too far way from their homes and leave them unguarded. As a result they invented the "buffalo calling ceremony" which was usually held during the winter months in hopes of luring the bison near to their villages. During the ceremony, which was presided over by the elders, the entire village became quiet. Dogs were muzzled and children were appeased with whatever it took to keep them quiet. Then everyone waited for the buffalo to come near to the village. Usually the plan worked, assuring the people that they were indeed being looked after by the Creator (Schneider, 1989: 62).

The Native concept of work correlates with the contemporary misguided notion of "Indian time." Observers often joke about "Indian time" as though to imply that First Nations are always late. The truth of the matter is that Indians are sometimes late (by non-Native standards), and sometimes they do not even show up for an appointment when they are expected to do so. This does not mean that a sense of time is always irrelevant, but rather that time per se is not the only nor necessarily the most important criterion by which to determine how a particular moment ought to be acted out. It is certainly not a top priority of itself. There are times when Indian people are actually early, depending on circumstances or purpose and the relative importance of an event. Above all, clock-watching per se simply does not happen. It is basically an irrelevant (and perhaps irreverent) entity in the Aboriginal scheme of things.

Traditionally, all tribal societies lived in tune with the cycles of nature. Living off the land and depending on its rhythms meant that nature dictated when things happened. No one went out to collect blueberries or other edibles until they had ripened to the optimal degree. Nor did they trap until the time of year when pelts were at their fullest. Crops were harvested when they were ready, not on a certain date. While they waited the hunters prepared or repaired their equipment and planned their strategies (Ross, 1992: 39). Thus the notion of "the time being right" is a principle embedded in the very nature of things; to dance to the tune of any different drummer would be foolish. Like the

Israelites, the First Nations well recognized who was in control of the elements. They reverently respected the Creator and were well aware of the consequences of neglecting His dictates. This is aptly illustrated in the reminder given to Israel by the Prophet Amos:

> . . . I also withheld rain from you when the harvest was still three months away. I sent rain on one town but withheld it from another. One field had rain; another had none and dried up. People staggered from town to town for water but did not get enough to drink, yet you have not returned to me, declared the Lord. (Amos 4:7-08)

## 4. Family Is First

> If anyone does not provide for his relatives, and especially for his immediate family, he has denied the faith and is worse than an unbeliever. (I Timothy 5:8)

The strongest unit among most tribal societies was the clan, a unilinear and usually exogamous kin-group (or sib), often characterized by matrilineal descent. Members of a clan lived together, including spouses and children, and were subject to a series of stringent regulations. In addition to being exogamous, clans usually had a set of names reserved for naming offspring, and their own burial ground. They often had special religious symbols, and their religious rites were carried out by specially designated individuals. Clans could adopt outsiders but they too would have to subscribe to clan regulations (Goldenweiser, 1968: 565f). Lowie (1956: 9) points out that among the Crow Indians, who were a matrilineal society, a person was always in the same clan as his or her mother but a man could never belong to the same clan as his children who were born into their mother's group. Even if a father adopted a child it automatically fell into the clan of his mother or that of the child's mother. Among the Crows a child could belong to the father's clan only if its mother married a man of her own clan, a practice forbidden by the rules of exogamy.

When Jacob (Israel), whose name became the tribal designation, relocated to Egypt he travelled with his entire household.

> All those who went to Egypt with Jacob – those who were his direct descendants, not counting his sons' wives – numbered sixty-six persons. With the two sons who had been born to Joseph in Egypt, the members of Jacob's family, which went to Egypt, were seventy in all. (Genesis 46:26-27)

Clans were (and still are) powerful units among member Nations of the former Iroquois League and the Huron Confederacy. West Coast Indians are also organized according to a highly complex clan system. Migrant Plains Indian tribes traditionally limited themselves to bands of fifty or a hundred souls in order to more easily move camp and follow the buffalo. More sedentary nations like the Arikara, Hidatsa and Mandan, organized larger village settlements of fifty or more lodges, albeit along strict family lines.

The Native orientation towards strong family linkages had many benefits. Child rearing, for example, was a family affair, and a responsibility shared by family and community. Education was ongoing, and consisted of elders telling stories, modelling and learning by doing (Haig-Brown, 1993: 38). Even today, in some tribes a significant portion of child-rearing is done by grandparents rather than parents. Often parents are quite young when they have their first child and they may need advice and assistance. Besides, it is an unspoken rule among Indians that age is correlated with, although not necessarily a direct cause of, wisdom. Grandparents are more settled, more relaxed about life, and therefore they are also more patient in child-raising. This inclination is also characteristic in sibling relationships. Older children in the same classroom are expected to help their younger siblings even though the uninformed teacher may see such actions as unscrupulous or cheating.

The Hebrew patriarch, Jacob had a son, Joseph, who was sold as a slave to Egypt by his jealous brothers who despised Joseph because he was his father's favorite. Despite this treatment, Joseph remained loyal to his clan, and when he eventually rose to a position of authority in Egypt, he remembered his father and arranged for him and his family to relocate to Egypt. There was famine in the land of Jacob so Egypt, which had plenty of food, seemed a logical place to live.

> So Joseph settled his father and his brothers in Egypt and gave them property . . . . Joseph also provided his father and his brothers and all his father's household with food, according to the number of their children. (Genesis 47:11a-12)

Clan loyalty had won out.

## 5. Giving, Not Receiving

> . . . the Lord Jesus himself said, "It is more blessed to give than to receive." (Acts 20:35b)

It is a common stereotype to conceive of Indian society as a sharing society. This is a "true" statement, depending on the context and meaning ascribed to the term. In a dictionary definition common to dominant society, "sharing" simply means that those who possess things or have access to resources may use those resources to assist others who may be in need. Implicit in the dictionary definition is the assumption that those who have resources may help out the needy if they so choose. The question of wanting to is seldom a relevant factor in Indian culture because of very limited individual choice in the matter.

The Indian twist to the definition of sharing leans quite heavily toward the obligatory component of the process, pretty much to the point that they who have, had better share. This tradition has deep historical roots. When a warrior returned from a successful hunt he was expected to give some of the meat to his immediate family members and relatives. In times of famine the meat was stretched out as far as possible. Rare was the warrior who refused to fulfil this obligation because there were strict, implicit rules about sharing. Conversely, there were also taboos about not fulfilling this requirement reinforced by various means of disapproval ranging from humor to outright shunning.

At the time of first European contact there were many formalized institutional approaches to sharing among North American tribes such as the potlatch, which was practised by West Coast Indians and the give-away dances sponsored by several Plains tribes. Joe Dion describes a particular give-away dance among his people the Crees in which a woman experienced such joy and euphoria during a dance that she virtually gave everything away. Her husband was away from home at the time and he was somewhat chagrined on returning home to discover that even his horse and gun had been "danced away" (Dion, 1996: 52). Today several tribes still practise the give-away dance at special occasions designed to honor individuals.

Some historians argue that the process of giving and taking was at least partially influenced by practices that arose at the time of first contact. As the fur trade got underway the First Nations were perceived as necessary allies in the enterprise and the fruits of their labors were a highly-valued commodity in the world market. When the markets eventually dried up and the Indian economy was faced with the inevitable need to change, the perception of the First Nations was radically transformed. Suddenly the Indian became someone who needed to be taken care of, the "white man's burden." There were even those who viewed the Indian Peoples with the patronizing attitude of admiring "the noble savage" with the wish to preserve Aboriginal cultures for posterity (Friesen, 1995a: 24).

By the mid 1880s the buffalo were wiped out and neither government officials nor the First Nations were prepared for the rather sudden disappearance the latter's food supply. They had envisaged that there would be an adjustment period during which the Indians gradually adapted to an agrarian model, planting crops and raising cattle. When these plans suddenly had to be modified the government simply concluded that they would temporarily help the Indians out by giving them rations. The Indians, on the other hand, projecting a more traditional stance in keeping with their philosophy, concluded that the arrangement would become permanent. Their "grandfather" (another name for the Indian agent) would look after them. Besides, how could a self-respecting warrior conceive of gaining a livelihood by scratching the ground with a stick and then waiting for things to grow (Dempsey, 1991: 42). This background set the stage for a long-term dependency relationship that has lingered to this day. As a priest in Fort Chipewyan, Alberta, once remarked to the author, "In the past we spent a lot of time teaching the Indians to receive. Initially, many of them were insulted by the process. Now, we wish to reverse the process and give them back their independence, and we are finding this a very difficult thing to do."

There is an element of a business-deal atmosphere to consider in this context which appears to have shifted to a dependency mode. Many Indian leaders have interpreted treaty benefits on a broader basis than the written conditions indicated. They see government grants and rations as a form of regular and perpetual compensation for the elimination of the buffalo and for lands taken. For this reason Indian people are sometimes advised by their leaders not to feel any measure of shame or chagrin for receiving welfare monies or other forms of government subsistence. These are strictly to be viewed as honorable and appropriate compensation for ceded territories and the right of unlimited occupancy (Snow, 1977: 28f).

Perhaps it was once the perspective of tribal societies to rely on their leaders to provide for their needs. The Hebrews had a dependency regard for their leader, Moses. They expected him personally to care for their needs even to the point of pestering him about their whims. When food or water were in scarce supply, they made a beeline to Moses' tent. At one point in their wilderness wanderings, when things were not going too well, they blamed Moses for taking them out of Egypt, the place of slavery (Exodus 14:11-12). Now they tried to convince Moses that it would have been better for them to have remained slaves than to die in the wilderness. They even considered electing a new leader and returning to Pharaoh's rule (Numbers 14:4).

Always the enduring and patient leader, Moses took all of the criticisms targeted at him and did his job. In one instance when Moses was away for a short time the people erected a golden calf to worship instead of Jehovah, but Moses, in the true form of a caring leader, pled with the Almighty to forgive them. Somehow, it was he who had neglected his responsibilities for their welfare.

So Moses went back to the Lord and said, "Oh, what a great sin these people have committed! They have made themselves gods of gold. But now, please forgive their sin – but if not, then blot me out of the book you have written" (Exodus 32:31-32).

## 6. Respect, Not Isolation

... in lowliness of mind let each esteem other better than themselves. (Philippians 2:3b KJV)

According to Cree elder, Joseph Couture (1985: 9), Native people possess a kind of self-reliance which non-Natives often interpret as uncooperative, stubborn, belligerent, impossible or even "dumb." Indians also act with an aloofness which is easily perceived as a reluctance to ask for or receive help other than in an emergency or crisis. Their live-and-let-live philosophy reflects at attitude of non-interference, for to interfere is to be discourteous, threatening or even insulting. Although group goals are paramount and individual identity is primarily awarded through community channels, the Indian community reveals a very strong tendency to avoid any form of direct confrontation with the individual.

The inherent difficulty in trying to understand this aspect of Indian philosophy originates in the European-inspired appreciation for talking things out. The Indian way is more inclined to stifle or repress issues or, if necessary to go beyond this point, find a means by which to handle the matter by avoiding direct confrontation as much as possible. Feelings are not to be shown, especially grief and sorrow. These are seen as emotions which, if indulged, can threaten the group, for they may incapacitate the person overwhelmed by them. Only when grief and sorrow are forgotten as quickly as possible can the group continue to meet survival challenges with the fullest attention and energy of every member (Ross, 1992: 29).

When some measure of confrontation between individuals becomes necessary, it is often accomplished by telling a story or by relating a legend. In this context, the purpose of storytelling is simply a means by which to let the second party know that his or her behavior has been inappropriate. The hearer is then supposed to figure out that he/she is the target of the story and is expected to amend his/her ways. If the point of the story is missed or if the listener perceives its purpose to be other than informing, another means may be sought to amend the situation. Usually this kind of undertaking is not attempted more than once. Parenthetically, when it is attempted on the uninitiated non-Native individual the scene can have quite humorous side effects. It is possible that non-Native listeners may become so engrossed in the story that they will make comments which clearly indicate their lack of awareness about what is transpiring. In one instance it did not occur to several individuals that they were the target of a particular story until one of them later related the incident to a third party. At that point the insight sparkled and the non-Native individual burst out, "Aha! This is about my behavior!"

In traditional Inuit society an indirect means of communicative was in effect so that one spoke only of oneself in a form of the second person. An announcement that one was going hunting was spoken thusly, "Someone wants to go hunting," or "Someone is going to the sea." Other everyday plans and behaviors were conveyed in similar style, "Someone is hungry, someone is angry, someone is going to bed," and so on.

Respect for the individual in the Native community is often practised to severe limits according to non-Native standards. For example, one woman removed her daughter from a particular school because the child, who was only seven years old, said she did not enjoy the school. After several days of absence the child was enrolled in another school. Similarly, when a Native truant officer visited a northern reserve home to determine why a ten-year-old was continually missing from school, the mother asked if the child was in school on the date of the visit. When the officer gave a negative response she simply replied, "Then I don't know. I told him!" The implicit belief is that if children are left to their own desires as much as possible, and not interfered with, they will develop both independence and a special loyalty to their parents.

Native people are not usually in the habit of providing extended answers such as those which exemplify non-Native explanations. Ask a non-Native why he or she was absent from an occasion at which they were expected to be present and an endless verbal harangue may result. Ask a Native person the same question and you may be rewarded with a one-word response or none at all. After all, if you respected the person, you would not even ask why they did not show up.

An Aboriginal leader observed recently that the Indian way relies heavily on effective early childhood education. Interpreted, this probably means that if Native children are correctly taught the old ways until they are six or seven years of age it will hardly ever be necessary to discipline them afterwards. This tradition has the advantage of encouraging children to become self-reliant and independent at a much earlier age than their non-Native counterparts. As such it is also a vital aspect of the philosophy of valuing and respecting individuality.

Most books about Indian ways mention that the traditional approach to child discipline, when it became necessary to implement it, was to avoid corporal punishment and instead to utilize humor, name-calling and ridicule as means of keeping individuals in line. In addition, the more informal means of social control were practiced by relatives or close friends, never by the parents. Doing so might jeopardize the bond between parent and child. In certain contexts today even non-Native people are expected to carry out these forms of discipline when necessary. If children become too boisterous, for example, and the non-Native person holds an accepted position such as a teacher, it will be expected that he or she will step in and bring order.

The Hebrew mode of discipline may have been a bit more strict, but they certainly valued children. Children were perceived to be a gift from God, and every Israelite woman longed to have children (I Samuel 1:20). Children were considered a blessing and a credit to the family (Proverbs 17:6), and they were seen to be the fulfilment of a Divine promise (Psalm 128:1-4). It was believed that children might be taken away from a couple in punishment if they violated God's laws (II Samuel 12:13b-14), and parents were believed responsible for raising children in the fear of the Lord. Parents were expected to be models and examples and to their children (Exodus 13:8), yet respect their individuality. Although the relationship of parents and children was morally closely connected, in the final analysis, all individuals would be judged on their own merits, that is, "Fathers shall not be put to death for their children, nor children put to death for their fathers; each is to die for his own sin" (Deuteronomy 24:16).

## 7. Community, Not Individuality

> And I will make of thee a great nation, and I will bless thee, and make my name great; and thou shalt be a blessing. (Genesis 12:2 KJV)

When Jehovah spoke these words to Abraham, the father of the Hebrew Nation, it set the stage for the development of a very strong ethnicity. The Hebrews now had a covenant with God, and if they obeyed His words, nothing or no one could stand in their way of being a conquering and prosperous nation. Moses warned his people about these conditions when he delivered them from slavery in Egypt (Deuteronomy chps. 1-4), and they were reiterated by his successor, Joshua, both at the beginning of his leadership (Joshua 1), and just before his death (Joshua 24). Other prophets like Isaiah (Chp. 42), Jeremiah (2:20) and Daniel (9:27), reaffirmed the promise of God's covenant from time to time, and Peter, Jesus Christ's chosen disciple, also made reference to it, reminding the Jews that

> Ye are the children of the prophets, and of the covenant which God made with our fathers, saying unto Abraham, And in thy seed shall all the kindreds of the world be blessed. (Acts 3:25 KJV)

Tribal societies like the Hebrews generally believed themselves to have a special relationship with the Deity, based partially on the grounds of tribal identity and longevity. Since the Creator had chosen them to dwell on this earth as a unique entity, obviously that meant something (Harrod, 1992: 38f). Many tribes historically also gave themselves unique names signifying their special identity in the scheme of things. The Blackfoot (the preferred term in the United States is Blackfeet) peoples also believed they were a covenant people and they braided their hair as symbol of this link with the Creator. They were firm believers in the Supernatural and, according to McClintock (1992: 167), they were subject to what were later called the Good and Evil forces that influence human affairs. Similarly, the Sioux believed that their Sacred Buffalo Calf Pipe, which had been handed down through the generations via the oral tradition, was the foundation of their religion. It too linked them with the Supernatural. Lame Deer (Lame Deer and Erdoes, 1972: 128) once noted sarcastically, "You white men killed your Jesus; we Indians haven't killed our peace pipe yet."

The Cheyennes still value their Sacred Arrows which were reportedly brought down to them from a Sacred Mountain in Wyoming called Devil's Tower (Looking Horse, 1988: 68). The Potawatomi hold a similar view about their sacred Chief Drum which to them is a symbol of a Divine link (Friesen, 1999: 208).

Belief in the importance of tribal identity downplays any notion of individuality as a separate entity. Any talents or gifts that an individual possesses must provide some benefit to the tribe or they are being misused. Any possession that individual may have must be available for use by any member of the community at any time. Traditionally, when a hunter was successful, his bounty was shared with everyone in the camp. If a vision quester was successful in his search, the blessings of his experience would be welcomed, validated and, hopefully, enhanced by and within the community. In the final analysis, the community, the people were what mattered, not individual attainment.

There is definite benefit in valuing community above individuality. As Lowie (1956: 329) points out, in the "olden days" of Indian culture, an individual was always better off in the company of his peers.

> A man may be a champion marksman, but when there is no game to shoot he falls back on the pemmican his wife has stored against that very emergency; and even in the chase he is most efficient when he hunts in company. His robes and leggings are the work of his wives or kinsmen; his very arrows are not of his own making but of the handicraft of skilled craftsmen. If he seeks renown, what are his chances as a lonely raider? Even a well-organized party was likely to be cut to pieces or be hard put to it when fleeing from superior numbers. Crisis lowered on every side, and it meant everything to be able to face life not alone but with a comrade shielded by one's family and clan, in the bosom of one's club.

There is an Old Testament account of an elder named Balaam who was hired by an outside tribe to curse his own people (Numbers 22). Balak, leader of an enemy tribe, feared the military power of Israel and thought to circumvent it by having one of their own elders curse them. Balaam apparently consented to do the horrible deed, probably for payment, but he was prevented from doing so by Divine intervention. On his way to the agreed site, the donkey on which he was riding was accosted by an angel whom Balaam was blinded from seeing. Eventually Balaam's eyes were opened and he realized the atrocity he was about to commit and promptly changed his mind. Then the angel spoke, warning Balaam to address Balak's people, but say nothing that would in any way defame Israel. This could have been the ultimate form of betrayal, but when Balaam did speak he could only utter words of blessing for his tribe.

## Conclusion

A comparison of tribal societies can ideally be accomplished only when similar histories are examined. As may be concluded from the foregoing discussion, Old Testament Israel and North American First Nations manifested very similar cultural inventories, ritualistic enactments and religious outlooks during their classic traditional times. Differences in practice began to emerge as development towards statehood occurred among the Hebrews. First Nations, however, maintained and still practice many aspects of their ancient tribal perspectives despite pressures to abandon their ways during the first few centuries of contact with Europeans. Unlike modern Jews, they have resisted the temptation to add the trappings of modern statehood and have clung tenaciously to the past. The Native cultural renaissance that began in the 1960s has strengthened the will among First Nations to revive traditional customs and bring them into the public domain. This motivation now affords observers an excellent opportunity to study components of Aboriginal theology and related practice that were heretofore kept secret. This possibility also allows interested observers to gain a deeper knowledge of First Nations' spirituality in a way that these insights can be compared with developing forms of state religions such as Christianity. Whatever the outcome, we must be grateful to the First Nations of North America for preserving so many of their ancient tribal ways. There is no doubt that a study of them offers a form of deep spiritual enrichment to the diligent observer.

# Five

# First Nations and Old Testament Israel:
# Theological Similarities

Social scientists characterize tribal societies as being of one mind, speaking with a distinct dialect and possessing a definite territory, and positing an homogenous and distinctive culture. Like other societies, these cultures traditionally operated according to a specific pattern which is the function of the integrated character of human beings who, as they incorporate cultural traits, sometimes very diverse in origin, organize them into viable ways of life (Mead, 1963: 14). The survival of such societies was traditionally possible because of their unified political organization and the strong sense of common solidarity they posed against any outside threat.

It is somewhat disappointing that scholars on occasion fail to note very definite similarities between different cultural configurations, thereby perhaps indicating a degree of bias towards one particular group over another. A case in point is the North American First Nation community whose traditional tribal beliefs and customs closely resembled those of the Old Testament Hebrews. Interestingly, many anthropologists with a Christian bias have also been quick to recognize the theological validity of Old Testament Jewish tribal customs as foundational to Christian culture, yet relegate that of North American First Nations to the pagan category. As the next two chapters will illustrate, an examination of the cultural milieu of both configurations, Aboriginal and Old Testament Judaism, will reveal a remarkable similarity between the two configurations and bolster the argument that First Nations theology has a rightful place alongside that of other world philosophical systems.

It must be emphasized, of course, that of themselves, cultural similarities between two groups do not imply unanimity of either purpose or structure. As Benedict (1934: 208) noted long ago, patterns of culture which resemble each other closely may not choose the same situations to handle in terms of their dominant purposes. This phenomenon is known to social scientists as the range of cultural alternatives available for selection within a given configuration, and should not overshadow the possibility of identifying meaningful cultural similarities. Conversely, it must also be noted that very few cultures handle their great occasions in any simple fashion, thereby strengthening the argument for cultural universals. Finally, the earmarking of similarities should in no way be perceived as anything more than the notation of parallels, and not in any way implying cultural or historical linkages. When significant similarities are noted, however, it must be acknowledged that the systems are of equal standing and deserving of further investigation.

# A Spiritual Orientation

## A Covenant People

One of the outstanding aspects of Old Testament Jewish history is their connection to the Creator via covenant. This kind of arrangement was probably not unique to Hebrew lore, but it is a frequently referred to item in their historical itinerary. The original contract appears to have been established during the time of Abraham, the father of the Jewish Nation (Genesis 17:1), when Abraham was ninety-nine years old. God promised Abraham that through his newborn son, Isaac, his numbers would increase and he would be the father of many nations. Later, this contract was renewed with Abraham's grandson, Jacob, when the latter had a vision about angels climbing up a ladder to heaven. At that point he built an altar of stones to commemorate the occasion (Genesis 28:18-19). When Israel attained nationhood under Moses' leadership the covenant was transferred to the people who were given ten commandments to obey as an indication of their faithfulness to the covenant (Exodus 34:10, 27; Deuteronomy 29:1f).

Jacob became heir to the Hebrew promise by cheating his brother Esau, out of the birthright. Jacob escaped his brother's anger by fleeing to his Uncle Laban's place. Years later, he sought a reconciliation with his brother and the two did eventually restore their relationship. Before his meeting with Esau, Jacob sought Divine approval for the encounter. First, however, he had to prove to himself that he was spiritually ready and he did this by wrestling with an angel for an entire day. During the struggle, Jacob turned out the socket of his hip. He named the place of the encounter, "Peniel," and retained a limp because of the ordeal he had experienced (Genesis 32:30). As a result Peniel became a sacred place to the Israelites and after that, out of respect to their leader, they refused to eat the tendon attached to the socket of the hip of any animal they butchered.

God's covenant with Israel was maintained when Joshua took over from Moses who had led the people out of bondage in Egypt. Joshua also erected a cairn of stones in recognition of the Divine covenant of Israel with the Creator (Joshua 8:30). He offered a sacrifice consisting of a burnt offering and a fellowship offering to the Lord on the rock altar. Then he copied the laws of Moses on stones and all the elders and people of the nation celebrated with him. In his final days Joshua prepared for his demise by summoning the leaders of Israel and reminding them of everything that the Lord God Jehovah had done for them, urging them to keep faithful to their end of the bargain they had made with God (Joshua 24:1f). During the period when judges governed the nation and initiated them into the promised land, the covenant was perpetuated on the basis of a message from God, "I will never break my covenant with you, and you shall not make a covenant with the people of this land ..." (Judges 2:2a). Israel was to eradicate the inhabitants of the promised land and not make treaties with them. Only when the resident nations were eliminated could Palestine truly be the land of God's people.

Agreements with God were usually confirmed by the building of an altar of stones and the offering of a sacrifice. The practice seems to have started with Noah who built an altar after the ark which he had piloted for several months landed safely on dry land. As the Bible has it,

> Then Noah built an altar to the Lord and, taking some of all the clean animals and clean birds, he sacrificed burnt offerings on it. The Lord smelled the pleasing aroma and said in his heart: "Never again will I curse the ground because of man ..." (Genesis 8:20-21)

Many Aboriginal peoples in North America also believe that their presence on this continent has been assured because of the special place they have in the heart of the Creator. An examination of the history of the First Peoples since European contact would seem to lend credence to this claim. Shortly after the turn of the twentieth century the First Nations were termed "the vanishing race," and predictions about their imminent demise abounded. By the 1930s, however, this trend had turned and the population of the First Nations began to grow again. Reasons for depleting populations among Aboriginal tribes included deliberate genocide by American troops, death from imported diseases to which the Aboriginal had no immunity, often spread by the distribution of infected blankets, and starvation after buffalo herds were deliberately annihilated. Enhanced growth began when the Aboriginal Peoples found alternative means of surviving, regained their spiritual foundations and developed immunity to imported diseases.

The fact of having an agreement with the Creator is a profound spiritual reality for Indigenous Peoples. According to the oral tradition of the Siksika (Blackfoot) Nation, often carried on to next generations via storytelling, the Blackfoot still braid their hair as a symbol that they have a covenant with God. As one means of differentiating them from other of God's creatures (animals), the Blackfoot people also received the gift of worship. This gift motivates a desire to "know more" of the Divine secrets which are often pursued via the vision quest. From the explorations of the vision seekers an idea of the order of the universe can be formulated. The conceptualized metaphor is that of a circle and every individual has opportunity to pass through various levels of the circle, which in turn lead to other spiralling circles, as one passes through life from birth to death. The braiding of the hair symbolizes the opportunity and commitment to learn as much as possible about the Creator's plan for one's life as one pursues this knowledge.

According to Wolfleg (1983), himself a respected Siksika elder, the Blackfoot were given a second indication of God's approval, symbolized by the ritualized burning of sweetgrass. After their world view was conceptualized the Blackfoot sought additional spiritual direction which was formalized by visions through the auspices of formalized spiritual societies. The people were given sacred medicine bundles which contained whole ceremonies to be used for specific purposes which included healing, hunting, teaching, warrior skills and other talents. Some of the more notable societies that promoted these gifts included the sacred Societies, Horn, Prairie Chickens, Crazy Dogs, Old Women, the Bees and Tobacco Society. Burning sweetgrass was a form of acknowledging the Creator's gifts to humankind. Accompanying prayers were said by the people as a group to indicate the corporate nature of this second covenant.

## Sacred Places

Although it is true that modern North American society recognizes virtually nothing of the sacred landscapes formally so regarded by traditional cultures like Israelites or Indians, there are still remnants of many sacred sites on this continent. Like their Old Testament Hebrew counterparts, many Indian tribes used natural phenomena such as rocks, trees, animal skins and animal bones in rituals to express their appreciation to the Creator. The Aboriginal people also attached spiritual significance to birds, animals, plants and solar bodies. Many sacred places revered by First Nations were ignored or desecrated by non-Natives after the Europeans arrived in North America. To this day there are still local and state governments who ignore AmerIndian pleas and continue to defile or destroy sacred hills or burial sites. All over New England one can find standing stones aligned with solstices or other celestial phenomena, stone "Indian forts," and stone embankments used for collecting the subtle currents of the landscape, and other places which are very much part of Native religious traditions (Verslius 1997:69). The Old Testament characters also erected multiple numbers of stone altars as places of worship, and their efforts were paralleled across the sea by the First Peoples of North America.

It seems ironic that many of the first visitors to this continent, many of them Christians, who no doubt deeply respected the religious efforts of Old Testament Israel, could so insensitively traipse over sites deemed hallowed by North American Indians. For the most part, the first Christian arrivals paid little attention to the Native American respect for the land. Even when Indian people did convert to Christianity, their traditional values, such as sharing, caring for the extended family and respecting the earth, were ignored. This unfortunate regard for what others held as sacred led to the destruction of many such places, such as a many ton boulder standing atop another in the woods of Massachusetts, as well as a sacred spring in Kansas known as Wakonda Spring. For years people of many tribal backgrounds came to the spring to present offerings. Hundred of effigy mounds, platform mounds and others with solar alignments were destroyed with no forethought of what they might have meant to the First Peoples. Serpent Mound, in southeastern Ohio, was badly vandalized before it was finally saved by the Father of American Archeology, Frederick Putnam, in 1881. Two rocks, atop a sacred mountain in Chaco Canyon in northwest New Mexico, marking out the summer solstice, were also targeted for damage, but escaped harm when the mountain was officially recognized as a historic site. Today archeologists are eagerly looking for special places that might have had significance to the First Peoples before European contact.

A familiar phenomenon across the plains are huge circles of rock formations known as medicine wheels, many of them with lunar alignments. The largest such formation is located on a mountain top, at nearly 10 000 feet altitude, in the Bighorn Mountains of Wyoming. This wheel is eighty feet in diameter with six cairns in its circumference and twenty-eight spokes emanating from the centre, marking numerous stellar alignments. Another significant medicine wheel, located at Majorville, Alberta, when excavated was found to contain nearly 3 000 artifacts. The exact meaning of the medicine wheels is not known, but the oral tradition clearly conveys the message that they had spiritual significance to the Indians who built them.

When Noah's ark finally came to rest on dry ground, he built an altar to the Lord in thanksgiving. This, the first such incident mentioned in the Scriptures, has often been held up by Bible teachers as an example and incentive for believers to do likewise. Oddly enough, when a similar action is undertaken by an Aboriginal person, using similar objects and with the same degree of reverence, to those same observers it somehow loses its validity. While the Old Testament Israelites continued to employ a similar physical inventory to that of the Indians when worshipping God, their Christian descendants believed that the erection of magnificent cathedrals was the best way to express their adoration of the Creator. The most elaborate edifice designed by the Old Testament Jews was a portable tabernacle in dimensions not unlike a huge teepee:

> Then have them make a sanctuary for me, and I will dwell among them. Make this tabernacle and all its furnishings exactly like the pattern I will show you. (Exodus 25: 8-9)

The tabernacle was an oblong rectangular structure with the interior divided into two chambers, inner and outer. The first chamber was the holy place or first tabernacle, and the second was the holy of holies where the Ark of the

Covenant rested. It was the place where the high priest offered an annual sacrifice on behalf of the people on the Day of Atonement. He performed his duties with reverence, in faith and with great precision.

By the same token, when the AmerIndian elder prepares for a sweat, even the most minute movement of everyone concerned has to be properly oriented. The practice of pouring water over heated stones to produce a cleansing steam bath is, of course, not unique to Indigenous peoples of North America. A similar practice was once quite common on several continents. As Bruchac (1993: 4) suggests, had the first Europeans to visit Mexico not been Spaniards but Scandinavians, they would have felt much more at home among the Indians because the Scandinavian use of the sauna much resembles the Indian sweat-lodge. The Mayan people, like the Aztecs, also made use of the sweat-lodge. Some of the Mayan temples had elaborate sweat baths made of stone, accompanied by stone-built hearths lined with potsherds, benches made of masonry for those taking a steam bath and drains built to carry off water.

Essentially, the North American First Nation sweat-lodge is a tiny, airtight hut, once primarily used for steam baths in areas where there were no streams for bathing. It is constructed by securing willow branches in the ground, tying them together at the top, then covering the dome-shaped structure thickly with brush, skins or old blankets (Underhill, 1965: 109). The principal parts of the sweat-lodge include the poles, the covering, the stones and the pipe. Each part of the preparation of the sweat-lodge has special meaning, and the sweat-lodge itself represents the womb. The willow poles form the structure of the device. Willow is perceived as representative of plant life and has a special relationship with water since it grows best next to a water source. Willow is also deemed to have the power of resurrection which is proven by the fact that it dies and is reborn by the process of losing leaves each year and growing new ones the following spring. Symbolic death is enacted by the individual who enters the sweat-lodge, and symbolically buries old unclean thoughts and is reborn by the regeneration of the ceremony.

The covering of the sweat-lodge was traditionally made of buffalo hides although today other materials are used. Once inside, the covering serves as the night sky, and when the opening to the sweat-lodge is closed, the inside becomes a living being. Within the lodge the individual becomes part of the body of something alive and very powerful. An important component of the interior is the selection of stones placed at the centre of the structure. Bruchac (1993: 36) emphasizes that the stones are treated with the utmost respect because each of them represents a unique characteristic. In some cases the number of stones and their arrangement may have occurred to the originator in a vision. Thus the stones are never thrown or dropped, and if one falls accidently while they are being carried from the fire to the inside of the lodge, it is replaced by another.

Finally, there is the pipe. Not all Native sweat-lodge ceremonies involve the lodge, but in the Lakota tradition, it is essential. The pipe is smoked within the lodge each time the doorflap is opened, and it is kept on the altar outside the lodge when the doorflap is closed. The pipe is very sacred to the Lakota people and its origins are steeped in the legend of White Buffalo Calf Woman.

For the AmerIndian, the sweat-lodge is viewed as a microcosm of the universe, and all living things are represented in its makeup – plants, birds, stones, air, water and fire. Each part of creation had special powers and these are available to the individual participating in the sweat-lodge ceremony. Among most plains tribes each of the four endurances of the ceremony lasted about ten minutes, and each represented a particular color, direction and inherent theme.

It is only a short philosophical leap from considering sacred sites to sacred objects and both the Aboriginal people and the wandering Israelites had plenty of these. For the Israelites, the Ark of the Covenant had great significance because it symbolized a constant awareness of Jehovah. The ark was a chest made of acacia wood, about four feet long, and two and one-half feet wide and two and one-half feet high. It was overlaid with gold inside and out (Exodus 25:11) and had a ring of gold at each corner through which poles were passed to carry it. The lid of the ark (the "mercy seat"), was made of gold and at each end of the lid was a cherubim made of hammered gold. The ark was originally built under the guidance of Moses who also supervised the placing of the two tablets of stone that contained the ten commandments into the ark. The ark served as a guide to Israel when they were traversing the wilderness, symbolizing the presence of God with them in their journey. At its presence the waters of the Jordan River parted (Joshua 3:11-17), and when it was carried around the walls of the City of Jericho (once each day for six days and seven times on the seventh day), the walls came tumbling down (Joshua 6:4-12, 20). Deemed a very sacred item by the Hebrews, only members of the priestly tribe of Levi were permitted to carry the ark (I Chronicles 15:2). At one point the ark was taken from the nation in battle but it was eventually brought back. At the return of the ark, King David announced:

> If it seems good to you and if it is the will of the Lord our God, let us send word far and wide to the rest of our brothers. . . . Let us bring the ark of our God back to us, *for we did not inquire of it* during the reign of Saul. The whole assembly agreed to do this, because it seemed right to all the people. (I Chronicles 13:2a, 3a, 4, italics mine)

The reverence with which the Ark of the Covenant was regarded is demonstrated by King David's suggestion that trial elders "enquire" of the ark (I Chronicles 13:3a). This tone suggests that the ark was considered a living entity, capable of communicating with those who consulted it. A similar tendency to revere inanimate objects is evident in the scene when the Jewish leader, Moses, ascended Mount Sinai to obtain the ten commandments from the Creator. While he was gone, his brother Aaron, the nation's high priest, seduced the people into donating all the gold they possessed which he then fashioned into a golden calf. The people then ". . . bowed down to it and sacrificed to it. . . ." (Exodus 32:8). It could be argued that Israel was influenced to idol worship by their interactions with neighbors they met and fought in the promised land, but their allegiance to the ark might suggest that they managed this perspective quite of themselves.

The penchant to afford allegiance to inanimate objects is virtually universal among tribal societies, and the North American Indians are no exception. Their view is a bit more complex, however, since they regarded all worldly entities as living beings with the potential to teach. This would include insects, birds, fish, animals, stones, plants, trees, and so on. One of the most sacred objects in use among Plains Indians particularly, were medicine bundles or pipe bundles. Harrod (1992: 68) explains the function of the bundles in this way:

> Medicine bundles, then, will be interpreted as complex symbolic realities which are associated with various dimensions of transcendent meaning. The ritual that surrounds these objects powerfully evokes a sense of these dimensions of meaning at both the level of individual experience and in the shared experience of the social world.

Medicine bundles consist of wrapped objects such as bones, skins or feathers encased in animal skin. In specifically describing the use of pipe bundles among the Blackfeet, Harrod (1992: 71) states:

> The material objects in the pipe bundle may typically include the following: At the center is the sacred pipe, often accompanied by the white buffalo headdress, both of which may be wrapped in red flannel. A number of other items may also be present, such as a smaller pipe for smoking during the ritual, as well as the skins of certain animals and birds, such as the owl, loon, swan, crane, muskrat, otter, fawn, and prairie dog. Tobacco will often be placed in the bird skins, and a rattle may be wrapped in the prairie dog skin. In addition, there are pouches containing paints, incense materials, and other items for use in the ritual.

Medicine bundles were representative of the vision which the original creator of the bundle experienced before assembling it. Subsequent owners may have added items based on their own experiences. Making the bundle and using it in the sense of "enquiring of it" made its message vital to the spiritual life of the tribe. Among the Blackfoot Indians medicine bundles could be purchased by other members of the tribe but only if the transfer of the bundle and its representative power or gift was approved by elders who traditionally opened it on occasion, particularly when a transfer of ownership occurred, and the protocol for doing so was quite specific. The centre teepee at the sundance camp was the location for such a ritual, and only people specifically invited to attend were permitted to do so. The ritual of opening a bundle began with the recitation of the origin narrative, preparing the participants for the ceremony to

# Historically Significant and

# Sacred Sites Among First

# Nations of North America

Totem pole featured in West Coast First Nations cultures carved by Tony Hunt incorporates the Hunt family crests: the raven; the double-headed serpent; the great grizzly bear of the sea holding a halibut; and between the serpent's two heads is a human figure. Victoria, BC.

Photos by Virginia Lyons Friesen and John W. Friesen

Buffalo herd, Bighorn National Park, WY. The park maintains a herd of this sacred animal, once deemed to be the "supermarket of the plains." The Plains Indians believed that eating the animal's meat would spiritually enrich the consumer.

Sleeping Buffalo Rock, east of Malta, MT. Traditionally local tribes sacrificed possessions to the Rock.

Buffalo Rubbing Stone, near Flaxcombe, SK.

Writing-on-Stone Provincial Park, east of Milk River, AB. The Blackfoot Nations believed that spirits occupied this area.

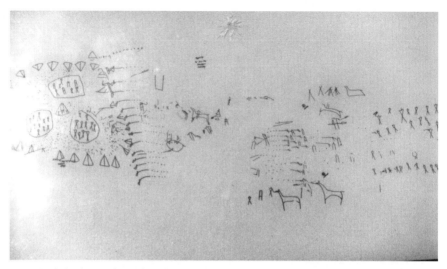

Artist's conception of ancient writings at Writing-on-Stone Provincial Park, east of Milk River, AB.

Chief Mountain, MT, sacred mountain to the Blackfeet Nation.

Medicine Rock at Gettysburg, SD. Considered sacred to the Lakota People, this forty ton boulder has imprints of human footprints, a hand-print and several animal footprints.

Medicine Wheel located at the east end of the Siksika (Blackfoot) Indian Reserve near Gleichen, AB.

Medicine Wheel (possibly Cheyenne), Bighorn National Monument, WY.

Crow Agency, MT "Teepee Capital of the World," site of the First Annual Indian Ecumenical Conference in 1970. Later conferences have been held on the Stoney Indian Reserve at Morley, AB.

Stoney Indian Park, site of the Annual Indian Ecumenical Conference on the Stoney Indian Reserve at Morley, AB, since 1971.

Nakoda Lodge, located on the edge of Lake Hector, across from Mount Yamnuska, sacred site of the Stoney Indians of Morley, AB.

Wanuskewin Heritage Park, meaning "Seeking Peace of Mind." The park is located on traditional Cree-Ojibway wintering grounds near Saskatoon, SK.

Mural at Tsuu T'ina (Sarcee) Elementary School, Tsuu T'ina Indian Reserve near Calgary, AB. Mural depicts separation of the Tsuu T'ina Nation from the Beaver Tribe. Legend has it that when the Beaver Tribe was on a river in northern Alberta, an old woman pulled on a protruding horn in the river and this action broke the river ice in half. Half of the tribe was left on each side of the crack. Those on the south later became known as the Tsuu T'ina Nation.

Original site of Chief Sitting Bull's (Tatanka Iyotake) Tomb at Fort Yates, ND. Killed and buried here in 1890, his body was moved to Mobridge, SD, in 1953.

Sacred Rock at Fort Yates, ND. The Arikara and Dakota Sioux believe that the rock resembles a seated woman wearing a shawl. Legnd has it that the woman was jealous of her husband's second wife and refused to leave camp when the tribe moved. A search party returned to find her and found that she and the child she held turned to stone.

Second tomb of Chief Sitting Bull, Mobridge, SD.

Burial site of Chief Red Crow, Blood Indian Reserve in southern Alberta.

Tomb of Geronimo, Apache Chief, Fort Sill, OK.

Site of the Battle of Washita, Cheyenne, OK. Here Chief Black Kettle, the "Peace Chief," and his family were massacred by Lt. Col. George A. Custer in a night attack.

Wounded Knee, Pine Ridge, SD. On December 29, 1890, the United States Army demanded surrender from a Lakota and Dakota encampment when an errant shot rang out. The army then massacred 250 Indians. Chief Red Cloud is buried at nearby Red Cloud Indian School.

Chief Crazy Horse Monument, Black Hills, SD.

Chief Crazy Horse Monument, Black Hills, SD.

On-A-Slant Indian Village (Mandan) – the "scaffold people," Mandan, ND. Sacred objects were sometimes stored on lodge rooftops. A sacred cairn was located at the centre of the village.

Serpent Mound, Locust Grove, OH. Centuries ago First Nations of North America built hundreds of mounds extending from the southeastern United States, north to Ontario, and west to the Dakotas. Purpose of moundbuilding was fourfold: effigy (like Serpent Mount), burial mounds, lunar alignments and temple locations.

Burial Mound at Mound City, Hopewell Culture National Historical Park near Chillicothe, OH.

Burial scaffolds, Ska-Nah-Doht Iroquoian Village near London, ON; part of a re-created Iroquoian cultural setting in southwestern Ontario dating about 1 000 years ago.

follow. Essentially, the ritual consisted of a complex of songs, prayers, dance and symbolic behavior intended to evoke horizons of transcendental meaning. Four major sequences governed the ceremony, each introduced by a set of seven songs, and if ownership of the bundle was transferred, the prospective owner's face was painted during the ceremony, marking him off from the everyday world and identifying him with meaning structures evoked symbolically in the ritual (Harrod, 1992: 75).

Closely related to the pipe bundle ceremony among the Blackfeet, albeit more complex in protocol, is the beaver bundle ceremony. Beaver bundles are much older than pipe bundles and go back to the time when the Blackfeet were a Stone Age people. Rituals connected with beaver bundles per se were always preceded by use of the sweat-lodge so that purification could occur. A smudge was prepared within the sacred teepee for additional cleansing; this involved the placing of sweetgrass on a hot coal and the fragrance of the sacred smoke filled the teepee during which the first set of songs were performed.

Contact with sacred objects was always restricted to certain individuals among tribal societies, an orientation that appears to have vanished in modern society. For example, the sundance of the Blackfoot Indians involved the role of a holy woman who initiated the ceremony. The ritual of the medicine bundle involved two women who were assigned the task of actually opening the bundle. They would approach the bundle in a series of four movements and on the fourth would unloose the tie that bound the bundle.

When the Ark of the Covenant returned to Israel during the reign of King David it was carried by ox-cart. At one point one of the oxen stumbled and it looked as though the ark might fall. One of the accompanying attendants, Uzzah, put his hand out to steady the ark and the Lord struck him down because he had violated the holy object. The punishment for violating the holy thing was death. King David was upset at God for striking Uzzah down, and he said so. When his anger abated he decided not to take the ark to Bethlehem, the City of David, because he was afraid he had gone too far in being angry with God. Instead he moved the ark to the house of Obed-Edom, the Gittite (I Chronicles 13:9-14).

Reverence for medicine bundles still persists among Native peoples, and most tribal members respect their presence with utmost devotion and not without a little fear. Some years ago, medicine bundles were placed in museums across the continent for safekeeping, but as the Indian spiritual revitalization movement has rapidly gathered momentum, some of the bundles have been retrieved. Museum curators have sometimes been reluctant to return the bundles, but when reminded of the severity of possible inflictions from violating sacred norms gradually they have been influenced to return them to their rightful owners.

## Ceremonies and Rites

In many ways the ceremonial life of North America's First Nations resembled those of other tribal cultures including Old Testament Israel. In such societies there was no distinction among the various facets of daily life – food gathering, religion, inter-tribal relations, politics, warfare, and so on. There was no one set of values for business negotiations and another for social intercourse or for worship. Everything was seen as interconnected and intertwined into what was called life. Being spiritual people, however, all activities and phenomena were perceived as spiritual in essence. If human behaviors were enacted in keeping with the laws of the universe, they would be right in nature. Special laws to designate certain behaviors as right or wrong were not needed. The true searcher would discover the rightness inherent in the workings of the universe (Kaltreider, 1998: 140).

Most Plains Indian tribes possessed a great deal of ritual, both public and private, which permeated all aspects of life. Most scholars are familiar with the seven sacred rites of the Lakota, for example, including the sweat-lodge, vision quest, ghost keeping, sundance, making of relatives, girl's puberty rite and throwing of the ball. Stolzman (1998: 21f) suggests that the making of relatives was not unlike a baptism ceremony and consisted of four major elements: (i) appropriate words said by a respected holy man; (ii) the taping of an eagle plume on the head of the person to be initiated; (iii) the singing of a ceremonial song; and, (iv) sponsoring a giveaway feast by the sponsor of the initiate.

The most significant Plains Indian ritual was probably the sweat-lodge which served to cleanse the individual to participate in other rituals such as the sundance or vision quest. There were also personal, private rituals which one might engage in after communication with a shaman, and like public rituals, were intended not only as a reflection of belief but as a means to expanding one's beliefs towards deeper meaning (DeMallie, 1988: 34). A successful vision quest, for example, could endow the individual with a supernatural aura resulting in the gift of healing or prophecy. When a vision quester returned from his vigil his claims about a vision were never questioned. As Curtis noted:

> The truth of the vision seen is never questioned; it may be wrongly interpreted, but always subsequent events will prove that the spirit-creature was not at fault. It follows naturally that a man never feigns to have seen a vision, for such a course could result only in misleading the people and thus bringing misfortune when the sages give their interpretation. (quoted in Gifford, 1976: 55)

The act of preparing oneself for possible spiritual blessing is also inherent in Old Testament offerings and sacrifices. The burnt offering, for example, described in the first chapter of Leviticus, symbolized an entire surrender of the individual or congregation to the Almighty. God's acceptance of the offering implied sanctification on the part of the seeker in a course of life that would be pleasing to God. The burnt offering was based solely on the assumption that Israel had been admitted to a covenant of grave with Jehovah, and so it could be offered only by those individuals who retained their standing in the covenant. The peace offering, described in the seventh chapter of the Book of Leviticus, was divided into three kinds – thank offering, votive (dedication) offering and freewill offering, and served to establish the Hebrews more firmly in the fellowship of Divine grace. The peace offering served to remind the people to be thankful for Divine mercies, much in the manner that the Crow Indians participated in a sweat-lodge ceremony as an offering of thanks to the sun (Lowie, 1956: 257).

In Old Testament Israel society one could also make a peace offering on an individual basis when impulse commanded, in fulfilment of a vow or in recognition of a special favor from Jehovah. Thanksgiving was not viewed by the Jews as a routine ritualistic act; being thankful was an attitude that was occasionally expressed in unintentional ways. The Psalmist says, "... give thanks to him and praise his name. For the Lord is good and his love endures forever; his faithfulness continues through all generations" (Psalm 100:4b-5). The Plains Indians would have agreed, and as a token of their perpetual thanksgiving, gratefully returned to the earth a portion of the meat of a slain animal both has an expression of thanksgiving as well as an acknowledgement of the interconnectedness of all phenomena.

Similar parallels may be drawn between two great ceremonies practiced by Israel and First Nations, namely the celebration of the Jewish passover and the Indian sundance (thirst dance). The passover was instituted to commemorate the deliverance of Israel from Egyptian bondage and the sparing of their first-born children when the death angel visited their camp. As the Psalmist states, "He provided redemption for his people; he ordained his covenant forever – holy and awesome is his name" (Psalm 111:9). The deliverance from Egypt was regarded as the starting-point for the nation of Israel. The prophet, Isaiah (43:14a, 15), echoed this thought, "This is what the Lord says – your Redeemer, the Holy One of Israel. ... I am the Lord, your Holy One, Israel's Creator, your King." Thus the Exodus from Egypt was viewed as the birth of the nation and the passover was its annual birthday celebration. In this sense it was also a celebration of a vow to remain true to God by fulfilling the requirements of the passover.

Of all ceremonies performed by the First Peoples of the plains, the sundance was probably the most publicized and the most misunderstood. Wandering bands of plains Indians gathered each summer to share news, socialize and celebrate their religious beliefs. Explanations regarding the nature and purpose of the sundance vary among its descriptors, but basically it was an expression of gratitude to the Great Spirit accompanied by prayers for a good future, health, strength and prosperity for the tribe. Snow (1977: 111) suggests that the purpose of the ceremony was "an expression of the joy and ecstasy of religious life, of being thankful for life, the beautiful creation, the rain, the sun, and the changing seasons."

In 1885, the Canadian government amended the Indian Act specifically to outlaw the sundance as well as the ceremonial distribution of property through potlatches practiced by northwest coast Aboriginal cultures in British Columbia. Encouraged by missionaries the government sought to hinder the practice of what were called extreme forms of behavior or rituals that showed the influence of the devil. The potlatch was described as an impediment to material progress and the sundance as a ritual of torture and self-mortification. Few investigators paused long enough to discover that the sundance was among other things ". . . primarily a thank offering to the Great Spirit, Kichie Manitou, for the re-awakening of all nature after the silence of winter" (Pettipas, 1994: 98)

Thank offerings are rarely made in today's technologically-driven society, but they may someday again be celebrated when the destructive conquest of the earths' resources has run its course and the search for renewal begins. Perhaps the long awaited reawakening of nature will occur in this millennium as human creatures of the earth begin to realize the necessity of presenting a thank offering to the Great Spirit in the form of respect for the earth.

# Six

# The Doctrine of God in Traditional Plains First Nations' Theology

If one understands the native religion of my people, it is not difficult to understand why so many of us embraced the gospel of Christianity. There was simply not that much difference between what we already believed and what the missionaries preached to us. What differences there were did not seem very important. (Chief John Snow, 1977: 17)

Although it is possible to generalize a fairly composite conceptualization of the Supreme Being known as God among the First Nations of North America, it might be wise to set parameters at the outset for this discussion. Principally, the basis for this discourse will be grounded in the Plains Indians configuration of the United States and Canada with particular reference to the Stoney (Nakoda Sioux) First Nation. The following paragraphs will outline the parameters of the field-work area in which these insights were gleaned.

For fourteen years my wife, Virginia, and I have been privileged to work with Morley United Church which is located on the Stoney Indian Reserve in Morley, Alberta. In this setting we have been both ministerial staff members and apprentices in Aboriginal theology. Many times we have been enlightened by the Stoney penchant to mingle theological truths with practical incidents. One Sunday morning, for example, the congregation was leaving the church when someone remarked what a beautiful day it was. As we glanced up to view the clear sky we saw an eagle circling the grounds. "Ah," said one of the elders. "The Creator is smiling on us. Good things will happen."

This incident led me to undertake a study of the Aboriginal concept of God and planted the seed for this book. I then set out to try to discover how First Nations perceive that Creator God reveals Himself and how He maintains contact with His people. During my search I have been encouraged by the extent of emerging literature on the subject, and my considerable contact with elders through the years has added a dimension of credibility to my search. As a result I am now convinced that there is a great deal of commonality between the traditional Christian concept of God portrayed in the Bible, and that held to by the Indigenous Peoples of North America.

## Off to a Bad Start

It is an intriguing enterprise to conjecture what might have happened if the first Europeans who arrived on this continent had come to discover instead of conquer. True, many history books suggest that the original invaders were pursuing both objectives, but in matters of spiritual concern, it is clear that their religious ethnocentrism effectively barred them from engaging in any meaningful investigation of Aboriginal belief systems. In short, they came to teach, not learn.

The rising interest in spirituality in North America is heartening to those of us who work in that arena. This curiosity has potential. When I arrived on the campus of the University of Calgary some thirty years ago, the topic of religion per se was taboo. Organized religion was particularly targeted for criticism, and any related conversation was subject to suspicion. The Vietnam War was in progress, hippies were conducting sit-ins at local parks and students were smoking grass as they raised serious questions about "the establishment"– which included the utility of the organized church. As the decades have unfolded, however, this sceptical perspective has been substituted by an interest in spiritual matters, oftentimes motivated and symbolized by New Age sympathizers. Although generally discredited by Christian theologians, that movement has at least helped spawn a renewed interest in the otherworldly aspects of human existence. True to the old adage that history repeats itself, last semester I was asked to teach a new course on religion in the Faculty of Education at the University of Calgary.

One of the more energetic pursuits of the proponents of the New Age movement has been emulation of certain practices inherent in the North American Indigenous Peoples' religious system, particularly the medicine wheel phenomenon. As previously mentioned, a medicine wheel is essentially a spiritual representation of harmony and courage. Physically, it consists of a central pile of rocks (or cairn) with spokes emanating in the four directions – east, west, south and north. Each direction has an inherent color, red, white, yellow and black. Each of the four spokes signifies a specific characteristic, a living creature, a season and an element, that is, the sun, the earth, night and fire. At one time dozens of these configurations could be identified across the plain but few remain.

Having personally visited a number of these sites, I can only marvel at their structure and intensity. Clearly they, like many of the Aboriginal religious rituals I have participated in, are illustrative of a highly developed religious system, each off which is rife with meanings and submeanings. For example, note Underhill's (1965: 108) description of one aspect of the sundance celebrated by Plains Indians:

At a Plains Sun Dance, the priest is to lay a rabbit skin at the centre pole in memory of a vow. It is a flimsy, grayish, little skin but he holds it in both hands as reverently as a different priest might hold a golden chalice. Three times he gestures towards the centre pole and withdraws. The uninstructed visitor grows impatient, for there is no pageantry to mark the importance of this event. But the Indian spectators know that the number four symbolizes perfection.

There are many similarities in both structure and function between Christianity and Aboriginal spirituality, although traditionally there were also significant tribal differences with regard to practice. Spence (1994: 359) appropriately notes, ". . . such a resemblance cannot be advanced as a proof that the divergent races at some distant period possessed a common mythology." What this resemblance does illustrate, however, is that the first missionaries might have saved themselves a lot of effort if they had taken the time to discover the fundamentals of AmerIndian spirituality if only to provide them with a more palatable and effective format by which to try to evangelize their new contacts. Evangelists always like to stress that an effective starting point in any such effort is to "know your target community." Unfortunately, North America's first missionaries did not have enough regard for Aboriginal rituals to even study their meanings, much less appreciate them. Tooker (1979: 31) observes that Aboriginal religious narratives have often been labelled "myths" by outsiders, but they are based on no less astute observations of nature than their European-derived counterparts, nor do they reflect any less intellectual effort than do the sacred and secular texts of the "high" civilizations of the Old World.

Porterfield (1990: 156) makes the point that when the European missionaries shared their versions of the Gospel, many Aboriginal prophets responded by incorporating aspects of the Christian faith into the structures of their rituals. After gaining some familiarity with the rudiments of the Christian faith, one Seneca prophet, Handsome Lake, postulated that his people understood and followed the teachings of the Gospel to a greater degree than those who imported the faith. He was particularly disconcerted to learn that the Euro-Christians who considered themselves God's people had crucified their own prophet, Jesus, and still perceived their religious practices to be superior to those of the First Nations. Despite this rather portentous deficiency, Handsome Lake, like many other prophets, tried earnestly to endorse the Christian faith and adapt its teachings to everyday life. Today many Native people simply combine elements of both their traditional way and Christianity into a personally workable faith.

## The Doctrine of God

A logical starting point for this discussion is to consider the question as to whether or not the Indigenous Peoples of North America traditionally believed in God. The answer is a qualified "yes." Smith (1995: 242) suggests that

Indians have always believed in God, but not in the sense that theologians do who adhere to EuroAmerican interpretations. At its core the Euro-American perspective focuses on individuality and conjectures that God is a separate, particular Creator Being who exists against the particular created universe. God is perceived in a "parent" role, and is usually elaborated in male form, that is, God, the Father. According to Smith, First Nations, on the other hand, believe in the Creator as a great Prevailing Force who resides in the sky. All brightness emanates from the firmament above and humankind and the eyes of humankind are dazzled by its splendor. Humankind therefore concludes that the abode of the Creator, the "Great Mystery," is the source of all life and of all spiritual excellence (Spence, 1994: 101-102).

Native North Americans in precontact days described God in terms of a universal principle instead of a determinate being one might call "God." This God may be perceived as an eternal spiritual Force characterized by presence and unity. This Force exists as a vital, energizing part of every living entity. Native Americans have always believed that by honoring the spirits of animals, for example, they are acknowledging the universal presence of the Eternal Spirit, not any particular form or separate entity. The concept of interconnectedness is also significant in this context because it implies responsibility to all living things. Traditionally, when an animal was killed for food it was the Blackfoot tradition to offer a prayer of thanks to the spirit of the animal for sustenance. A portion of meat was then buried in the ground to honour the interconnectedness of all things. The Sioux believed, "We are all related to all things" or, "we are all related – we are all relatives" (McGaa, 1995: 9). Since a very fundamental plank in Indian philosophy mandates caring for one's relatives, and sharing with them whatever resources one has, by parallel argument it also means that one has a responsibility to the earth and to every living thing, animate or inanimate.

One key difference between Indigenous theology and EuroAmerican-originated creeds may be illustrated with reference to the interpretation of John 3:16a, "For God so loved the world that he gave . . ." To First Nations this simply means that God (the Force) created and provides for the earth in all facets, as a complete entity. EuroAmerican Christians, on the other hand, will interpret this passage to mean that God loves and gives to people, but not necessarily the other living entities He has created – at least not in the same sense. As Tinker (1996: 156) notes,

> The danger of such privileging of human beings should be obvious. It runs the risk of generating human arrogance, which too easily sees the world in terms of hierarchies of existence, all of which are ultimately subservient to the needs and whims of humans.

Earmarking nonhuman forms of life as inferior minimizes responsibility towards other life forms and often justifies the abuse of animal life as well as the earth's resources. In this context it is easier to appreciate the implied universe stewardship inherent in Aboriginal theology.

As an addendum, it might be mentioned that some Aboriginal observers conceptualize the workings of Mother Earth as a unity. The Great Sioux leader, Black Elk, perhaps because of Christian influence, identified the Great Spirit as a governing force with authority over everything and synonymous with the God of the white man. Porterfield, (1990: 159) suggests that Black Elk ascribed to the workings of the Great Spirit parameters that included all things: the trees, the grasses, the rivers, the mountains, and all the fourlegged animals and the winged people. Black Elk's God, therefore, is more than a governing force; He is the Creator and Life Force within all things.

Until recently, most Christian theologians viewed the ecological concerns of Indigenous Peoples as corollary to the Christian stewardship obligation. For Indian people, however, the belief in God mandates an inherent admonition to respect the earth, which may be perceived as our natural "mother" (Cajete, 1994). The "parents" of humankind, the Great Spirit and Mother Earth (who are essentially a unity), have provided their children with all of the resources needed to sustain and perpetuate life. If properly guarded, respected and cared for, Mother Earth will provide plenty of food, water, shelter and resources for other needs for all generations to come. In light of the many recent incursions into sacred territory for destructive purposes, that is, the abuse of the earth, Native leaders are deeply concerned that the corruptions of western society will permanently harm Mother Earth. This abuse clearly violates Christian responsibility and displeases the Creator.

## A Personal God?

Stolzman (1998: 182f), a Roman Catholic pastor and theologian, has observed that some AmerIndian spiritual leaders object to the EuroAmerican tendency to describe God in anthropomorphisms. Stolzman makes the claim that Native elders prefer to depict God in strictly abstract, philosophical and theological terms which he calls "third-order abstractions from reality" in the sense that they are always deficient in some reality. Stolzman suggests that First Nation theologians deliberate on the assumption that the more simple and abstract a term is, the more spiritual it is. He disagrees with this assumption, arguing that cognitive distinctions examine the materiality of phenomena, rather than their spirituality. This is why cognitive examinations of God always end up in paradoxes. True to his Roman Catholic attachments, Stolzman postulates Jesus Christ as the total, real anthropomorphization of God and the model for all Christians. This belief mandates evangelistic efforts among peoples who possess only a shadow of the Gospel truth, that is, anyone whose experience of the Almighty varies with this interpretation.

Stolzman may be correct that Aboriginal conceptualizations of God are abstract and fuzzy, but this perspective apparently does not diminish the feasibility of belief in incarnation. The Blackfeet, for example, have a legend of Poïa, who was sent to earth as Star Boy by the Sun God for the purpose of instructing the Blackfeet in worship. After establishing the ceremonial of the sundance, Poïa returned to the home of the sun and became a morning star (McClintock, 1992: 491). Similarly, the Micmac believe in an incarnate being named Glooscap who reportedly came to earth to transform animals into their present shapes and teach his people how to make a living. Glooscap travelled a lot while he was on earth, spoke all languages and made friends with the animals. He had control of the elements and could make the sun shine or the rains fall at will, much in the manner that Christ stilled the storm (Mark 6:51). When Glooscap's work was done, he left the earth but promised to return whenever the people had need of his guidance (Friesen, 1997: 54).

Most Plains Indian tribes traditionally postulated a similar concept of a "middle kind of god" like Glooscap. The Ojibway called him Nanabush and believed that he came to earth to arrange things in order, that is, the shape of animals and the landscape of the earth. Like the parallel being postulated by many other tribes, in the form of the Trickster, Nanabush served a somewhat ambiguous function both as benefactor to people and as a self-indulgent and rather aimless wanderer (Miller, 1995: 108).

Native notions of incarnation basically parallel the Christian concept of Jesus Christ as the sent Son of God who was to interpret God's will to humankind. If their perception of God, the Great Mystery was vague, there was less doubt about the role of their envisaged intermediary figure. Perhaps these similarities explain why so many Indian tribes so readily accepted the Christian Gospel when it was first presented to them.

## Individualization of Faith

While much of traditional AmerIndian religious life was community-oriented, a special place for the individual was set aside in the system – particularly in the context of religion. The notion that the Great Spirit has traditionally been perceived by First Nations theologians as a universal Force or Presence may lead some observers to conclude that any form of individual contact with the "Grand Force of Being" would be impracticable. On the contrary, there is ample evidence that in Aboriginal thinking individual human contact with the Divine was not only considered a legitimate pursuit, but it was both sought after and often realized. Central to the process was the vision quest.

When they reached a certain age, depending on their tribal affiliation, young men volunteered or were selected to isolate themselves from their communities (usually for four days), during which time they would seek to make contact with the Great Spirit. There were also tribes who selected both men and women for this assignment. The possibility of the success of the process was enhanced by the participant refraining from any form of nourishment and maintaining an attitude of prayer. He was also carefully tutored by an elder who oversaw the process. Among plains tribes the practice was that a young man would repair alone to a hillside or canyon top and pray that a guardian spirit would be revealed to him. Should the experience prove to be successful, the youth might experience a visit by the spirit of an animal or bird and, if so, could later consult with it whenever he felt the need to do so. Such visitations were seen as an awarding of spiritual power, insight or gift which was respected by the community.

The biblical parallel with vision quest may be seen in the frequent solitude of those who were or later became prophets. Moses, for example, was tending sheep in the desert when he saw a burning bush that was not consumed by the fire. His trance resulted in his recognition of the locale as "holy ground" (Exodus 3:5). Elijah was in a depressed state when he fled from Ahab's forces on Mount Carmel and hid in a cave. His vision included wind, an earthquake, fire and a gentle whisper (I Kings 19:11-13). When Elijah emerged from the cave he encountered Elisha who recognized the call of the Lord in Elijah's words and indicated that he was ready to heed them. Amos, the shepherd-turned-prophet, envisaged a swarm of locusts, fire and a plumb line while on duty, and he felt compelled to share a message of judgement with his people (Amos 71-8).

The biblical men of message were not necessarily seekers of visions, but messages from God came to them nevertheless. Saul (who later became the Apostle Paul), was on the Damascus road when he was stricken with a flashing light and addressed by a voice from heaven (Acts 9:3-4). The experience changed the course of Paul's life so that his authority to plant churches and write essays that later became scripture was deeply respected by the early apostles. True, he had some disagreements with the Church Council at Jerusalem about wanting to convert Gentiles (Acts 15:5), and with Barnabus about the selection of missionary personnel (Acts 15:38-39), but Paul's reputation survived both of these incidents.

The perception of dreams as valid forms of Divine message is crucial to both biblical interpretation and understanding of Aboriginal theology. Chief Red Crow of the Blood First Nation once had a dream in which a gopher spirit came to Red Crow and said that if he put a blade of grass in his hair every time he went to battle he would never be hurt. Red Crow did as he was advised and although he was engaged in nineteen battles, he was never harmed. Biblical instances of special dreams are numerous, some of them paralleling the warning element in Red Crow's experience, for example, God warned Abimalech (Genesis 20) and Laban (Genesis 31:24) through dreams, and because of her dream the wife of Pilate cautioned her husband out of concern that harm might be meted out to the "Just One," namely Jesus Christ (Matthew 27:19). Other New Testament examples include Joseph being advised to take Mary as his wife (Matthew 1:20-21); wise men (elders) being warned to return to their country another way (Matthew 2:12); Joseph being warned to flee to Egypt to avoid Herod's wrath (Matthew 2:13), and his being told to return to Israel after Herod died (Matthew 2:19-20). The Apostle Peter was also the recipient of a vision in which he saw ". . . all kinds of four-footed animals, as well as reptiles of the earth and birds of the air . . ." (Acts 10:12) signifying that God is no respecter of race, creed, religion or culture. Peter needed a little coaching in interpreting his dream, but Cornelius, also the recipient of a vision, was the man for the job. The end result was that Peter's view was quickly enlarged to realize that "God does not show favouritism" (Acts 10:34). If only contemporary theologians could make appropriate biblical interpretations so adroitly.

Despite the reluctance of contemporary biblical scholars to validate dreams and visions as legitimate forms of Divine contact, in his address at Pentecost the Apostle Peter felt sufficiently enlightened to quote the prophet Joel:

> In the last days, God says, I will pour out my Spirit on all people. Your sons and daughters will prophesy, your young men will see visions, your old men will dream dreams. (Acts 2:17)

Contemporary Christian theologians might not wish to be as literal as Peter, backing up their scepticism with allusions to the fact that none of the epistles make mention of either dreams of visions. Indigenous elders are not so easily put off, and they expect that the Great Spirit always finds ways to communicate special messages to His children.

## Role of Prophets and Elders

In traditional Indian culture males were often recognized for their talents as hunters, warriors or guides, but to be properly executed even these enterprises required a form of spiritual confirmation. This enactment was the responsibility of the shaman or elder, whose office was not one of appointment but of informal recognition. As Beatrice Medicine (1987: 141), herself a Lakota Sioux elder, explains, elders are ". . . those people who have earned the respect of their own community and who are looked upon as elders in their own society."

It is useful to differentiate several kinds of shamans or elders who were operant in traditional in First Nations context. A wide range of gifts were recognized for that office, that is, there were individuals who were recognized as elders because of their special insights pertaining to medicines, leadership, spiritual knowledge or other areas. These individuals might apprentice to themselves young people who would hopefully inculcate this special knowledge through an unspecified period of time, on a one-to-one basis. That way the unique gift of knowledge held by the elder would safely be transmitted to the next generation. The elders of which Professor Medicine speaks are men and women of wisdom, so designated because they have demonstrated unique insights, and can perhaps offer relevant, insightful prophetic utterances. Meili (1992: xi) describes her experiences in consulting with elders:

> I was impressed by their prophetic vision. . . They taught me that I am part of God, so I could stop my search in trying to find Him/Her in someone else. . . . the Great Spirit, or life, or God (whatever you consider to be the highest), is love and always says yes if we seek it and try to live good lives. The elders collectively taught me that all things have a spirit and gently influenced me to give up the search for personal enlightenment and gain. I need to love, trust, and learn from all my relations.

Psychologist and Cree elder, Joseph Couture, points out that elders often serve as mediaries or spiritual therapists in assisting seekers to grasp the Divinely-designated roles they should play in this life. For example, consider the following elder sayings:

> Don't worry. Take it easy. Do your best. It will all work out. Respect life. Respect your elders. It's up to you. You have all the answers within you.
>
> Listen to what Mother Earth tells you. Speak with her. She will speak to you. (Couture, 1991a: 205)

Native elders often also play an interpretive role as the following recommendation by the late Charlie Blackman, an elder of the Chipewyan Nation, reveals:

> On a given day, if you ask me where you might go to find a moose, I will say, "If you go that way you won't find a moose. But, if you go that way, you will." So now, you younger ones, think about that. Come back once in a while and show us what you've got. And we'll tell you if what you think you have found is a moose. (Couture, 1991a: 205)

Clearly the pursuit of the "moose" metaphorically represents the individual's search for personal meaning, purpose and destiny. Initially, an individual may seek out an elder for guidance regarding a potential direction to undertake in seeking personal fulfilment regarding a life goal. The elder invites seekers to check in from time to time in order to help them evaluate whether or not they are indeed on the moose's trail.

Biblical examples of consultation with elders/prophets are ample. King Saul violated good sense when he bypassed the prophet Samuel's advice while the latter was alive, then took it upon himself to visit Samuel's ghost with assistance of the witch of Endor (I Samuel 28). Naaman, a commander of the army of a neighboring nation of Aram, sought out the Hebrew prophet Elisha about the latter's gift in healing (II Kings 5:1). The prophet, Nathan, dared to offer guidance to King David without being requested to do so. During their encounter it became obvious that David had strayed so far off course that he failed to recognize himself as the principal offender in a legend related by Nathan. In David's case one could say that he was hunting the wrong moose

(II Samuel 12). Jesus Christ Himself fulfilled the role of elder when He queried His disciples about His identity. "Who do people say I am?" (Mark 8:27). When their response indicated the need for further clarification He continued, "But what about you. . . . Who do you say I am?" (Mark 8:29)

The need for spiritual assistance from individuals whose gifts are have been recognized and confirmed by the family of God is deeply implanted in both Aboriginal and Christian traditions. This too, could have been an encouraging discovery by North America's first missionaries if they had been in less of a hurry to pursue the moose of planting foreign flags.

## Structures to Bolster Belief

Traditionally, the Plains First Nations of North America had neither formal church congregations nor permanently-designated worship centres. Wherever they travelled in search of the buffalo, however, their portable temples went with them. When the Sundance was sponsored, the teepee at the centre of the camp was designated as the high place of worship while the ceremony was being held. When the sundance was over, religious rites and rituals were in the hands of elders who governed the spiritual welfare of the people.

Today ample literature is available about formalized religious structures among the First Peoples in most parts of North America before and immediately after first contact. The fundamental spiritual purpose and meaning of many of these structures, however, have only recently been brought to light, thanks to Aboriginal writers. Early North American scholars who spent time in First Nation' communities made numerous observations about aspects of their lifestyle have been helpful in passing along rudimentary knowledge of AmerIndian religious structures. These have recently been supplemented (and perhaps even corrected) by Aboriginal writers. In eastern Canada, for example, inside knowledge about the Midewiwin has recently been made available thanks to two principal works by Ojibway scholar, Basil Johnston (1988 and 1995). Essentially the Midewiwin comprised a group of esteemed spiritual leaders who were in charge of maintaining and developing all aspects of Ojibway medicinal-religious practices, and it took years of instruction for an initiate to master four calibrated levels of knowledge. The Plains tribes also featured formal societies known as sodalities whose responsibility it was to preserve and pass along revered knowledge that was translated into songs, rituals and ceremonies (Friesen, 1997: 132).

Moving away from the plains region per se it is possible to affirm the establishment of formalized religious edifices among North America's First Nations, particularly among moundbuilding cultures of the southeastern states. Before 1492, moundbuilders in this region amassed thousands of piles of earth into effigy formations and as temple foundations or as burial sites. These earthen edifices were plentiful in regions from the Great Lakes in the north to the Gulf of Mexico in the south; from the eastern portions of the Great Plains to the Appalachian Mountains. These were impressive structures, and constituted the most conspicuous record of prehistoric American Indian culture to be found on the landscape of eastern North America (Woodward and McDonald, 1986). The first European viewers naturally assumed that a people other than the First Nations had built them, but gradually archeological proof emerged to show that the builders were native to the area. Central to their culture was a form of organized religion, epitomized in the form of elaborate temples built on carefully-constructed mounds.

The four corners region of the southwestern United States which touches the states of Arizona, Colorado, New Mexico and Utah was once home to an ancient people known as the Anasazi (the "Ancient Ones"). Ancestors of many of the modern pueblo peoples, the Anasazi built huge stone and mud-walled cities into the walls of canyons in the four corners area. Central to their lifestyle was a circular construction designated as the "kiva," which was the site of religious instruction for selected youth as well as for ceremonial practice. Today, for example, members of the Hopi Nation, who are descendants of the Anasazi, still practise many of the old rituals and ceremonies, and it requires four years of careful instruction before a would-be priest is approved to celebrate these traditions (Friesen, 1993).

Those First Nations who chose to develop elaborate physical religious structures were usually non-nomadics, and it is probably safe to conclude that the buildings they erected for these purposes were primarily functional rather than ornate. They were utilitarian, and intended only to supplement the essential function of contacting, communicating with and worshipping the Creator, the One True God. Like their plains counterparts, who took their portable temples with them, these First Nations were seeking the very same God on whom the incoming Euro-Christians thought they had a monopoly.

# Seven

# Theological Comparisons and Contrasts:
# Anthropology and Epistemology

The previous chapter dealt with what is probably the most fundamental topic in theological deliberations, namely perspectives on the existence and nature of God. This discussion of two additional major doctrines will rely on conservative New Testament Christian hermeneutics as a point of departure in contrasting North American Aboriginal perspectives. As will be shown, conceptually there are many points of similarity between the biblical perspective and First Nations' theology even though the language may vary somewhat. Again, had the first missionaries to North America made note of this it might have lent a new direction to their efforts in evangelism.

## Anthropology: God's Relationship to Humankind

One of the basic anthropological questions frequently debated by theologians has to do with transcendence versus immanence. On one hand, the Creator relates to humankind as the Transcendent One, that is, God is self-sufficient apart from the world. He is above the universe, yet comes to the universe from beyond. On the other hand, the Creator also relates to people as the Immanent One; He is present to creation. He is active within the universe and is involved with the processes of the world and in human history. As the Apostle Paul put it, ". . . he is not far from each one of us. For in him we live and move and have our being . . ."(Acts 17:27b-28). Most European theologians have traditionally come down on the side of transcendence, while First Nations theologians have emphasized immanence.

Basic Christianity accepts the Old Testament proposition that the creation of humankind was the Creator's idea (Genesis 1:26). From the initial creating act of man and woman, God "hath made of one blood, all nations of men to dwell on the face of the earth, and hath determined the times appointed, and the bounds of their inhabitation" (Acts 17:26 KJV). The implications of the phrase "of one blood" has led to many interpretations, and some of them could even be labelled deviant in an effort to justify the notion that all races are not created equal.

The similarity of First Nations' accounts of creation and the great flood are similar in nature to that rendered in the Book of Genesis, that is, "In the beginning God created the heavens and the earth. . . . And after seven days the floodwaters came on the earth. . . . And rain fell on the earth forty days and forty nights" (Genesis 1:1, 10, 12). The Blackfoot account is somewhat parallel; note the resemblance to the story of Noah. "During the flood the Old man was sitting on the highest mountain with all the beasts. . . . After the flood, the Old man mixed water with different colors. He whistled, and all the people came together" (Wissler and Duvall, 1995: 19). In the Assiniboine version when the flood came the people were told to go up on a high mountain, take four logs, build a lodge and wait out the deluge (Fort Belknap Education Department, 1983: 2). The Cherokee creation story reveals somewhat familiar elements.

> In the beginning all living things lived and dwelled above in the sky we know. . . . At the first, earth was very flat and soft and wet. . . . Birds were sent down to see if the earth was dry enough to live on. . . . When the earth was finally dry and the animals came down, it was very dark. . . . They placed the sun in the sky to give them light and set it so it would go across the island every day from east to west. (Coffer, 1978: 43-44)

The lore of many North American Indian tribes emphasizes creation accounts as particularly important. Flood stories are frequently included in the tribal cultural repertoire revealing similar elements to the Judeo-Christian account. The creation story of the Cheyenne states that after the Creator had made firm ground He took from his right side a rib and made it into a man. From the man's left side he took a rib and made a woman. These two persons now represent the southern and northern Cheyenne tribes respectively (Grinnell, 1971: 242).

Like Hebrews and Christians, the Indigenous Peoples believe that the Creator designed the world for His creation to dwell on and to enjoy. He endowed the earth with ample forms of sustenance and required only that his "subjects" honor the earth and take care of it, that is, "The Lord God took the man and put him in the Garden of Eden to work it and take care of it" (Genesis 2:15). Significantly, a covenant was made between Creator and created which stipulated that in return for adherence to belief in Him and conformity with His expressed will, humankind would be succoured and enriched in this life and admitted to eternal salvation in the next world (Zentner, 1972: 89).

In the biblical account of creation the trouble began when humankind fell from grace and disobeyed God's plan for a peaceful and complementary world. This is known in Christian lore as the fall of humankind or, the story of Adam and Eve. In Aboriginal versions there is no direct reference to the fall of humans, but it is implied in the fact that humankind is innately powerless and constantly cries out to be pitied when confronted with life's unconquerable vicissitudes such as danger, famine or the unexplainable. People's relation to creation is always such that they must submit themselves to the rhythms of nature. By crying out to the Creator people can at once address the sum total of supernatural help which is always at their disposal. People must, of course, purify themselves if they expects to receive Divine approval. The sweat lodge ceremony epitomizes the cleansing process.

Among the Sioux the purpose of taking a sweatbath is "for one's life," that is, the primary focus of the event is upon the life of the people. Bruchac (1993: 11) identifies two basic types of sweats that were in use in North America at the time of Europeans arrival on this continent. One type was the vapor bath which involved heating stones in a fire outside a lodge. The stones were then carried inside and the lodge was sealed. Water was then poured onto the rocks and the process created steam. The second type of sweatbath consisted of dry heat created by a very warm fire in a sweat house which caused those within the house to sweat. The heat was almost as intense as that created in the vapor bath, and dwellers in the latter type of sweat house could use the house as a dwelling or as a ceremonial house on a continuing basis. Among the Inuit, respirators made of fibres were often used during sweats to prevent burning of throats and lungs because of the intense heat (Bruchac, 1993: 11).

The cleansing process of the sweatbath is intended to assist participants in seeking Divine guidance for healing of others, protection of the young and the old, and material help and strength for some personal or family goal (Stolzman, 1998: 44). As a result of this advantage, humans have a daily duty to perform supplication with the Creator (Powers, 1977: 46). As Charles Eastman (Ohiyesa), the Santee Sioux elder, put it, "In the life of the Indian there was only one inevitable duty – the duty of prayer, the daily recognition of the Unseen and Eternal" (Seton and Seton, 1966: 18). Prayer was offered as thanksgiving for supplication and indirectly for forgiveness. The virtues to be lived out in daily life included care of the physique, cleanliness, bravery, cheerfulness, honesty, kindness and peace. Although many tribes did not have a word that could directly be translated as "sin," trespass was seen as disregarding the laws of the Spirit. When trespass had been committed, in order to regain favor with the Creator, or with the tribe for that matter, certain redemptive-like rituals had to be enacted.

A key difference between the contemporary Christian perspective and North American Aboriginal conceptualization is with regard to the relationship of humankind to nature. Traditionally, there was no philosophical distinction between the two views. According to the Judeo-Christian tradition, man was originally placed in the Garden of Eden "to work it and take care of it" (Genesis 2:15). This mandate does not create a problem in the Aboriginal interpretation if it means that the processes of nature are to be respected. The Hebrews, of course, were in the business of "subduing the land" in the sense of taking possession of it from their enemies (Numbers 32:22, 29; Joshua 18:1; I Samuel 7:13; I Chronicles 22:18). There is no particular instruction in the Bible to Israel that they should subdue the earth in the sense of exploiting its resources to the point of permanent infertility. The New Testament also endorses the concept of respecting the earth, for example, in the prophetic Book of the Revelation: "Do not harm the land or the sea or the trees until we put a seal on the foreheads of the servants of our God" (Revelation 7:3). The Book of James also addresses the matter of humankind's relationship to the earth using the example of the farmer: "See how the farmer waits for the land to yield its valuable crop and how patient he is for the autumn and spring rains" (James 5:7b). Nowhere is it implied in Scripture that the ruthless disregard of the earth's natural processes is appropriate. The Scripturally-mandated attitude is to remember that "Everything God created is good, and nothing is to be rejected if it is to be received with thanksgiving, because it is consecrated by the word of God and prayer" (I Timothy 4:5).

The interpretation that exploitation of the earth is Divinely sanctioned or at least tolerated may have been spawned with the advent of the Industrial Revolution or by the emergence of the Protestant work ethic during the Protestant Reformation. The emergence of the scientific age and the related discoveries proved that increased yields could be squeezed out of the earth with increased chemical usage with complete disregard to the long range effects of such an approach. The guilt of this desolation of the earth must be shared by everyone who mismanages the resources of the universe or who consciously or even inadvertently benefits therefrom. The assignment of guilt, however, will not assuage the problem, but a new sense of appreciation for what we have left could be a good starting point.

## Epistemology: The Content of Theology

Like their tribal counterparts, the Old Testament Hebrews, traditionally the Aboriginal peoples lived according to the oral tradition. Their creed was aptly summarized by the psalmist: "I have hidden your word in my heart that I might not sin against you" (Psalm 119:11). Although it is commonplace to juxtapose the values and merits of the oral and written traditions, there are many examples in history which illustrate the indisputable reliability of the oral tradition even though defenders of the written tradition might not agree. They also might not want to learn that there are many examples of recorded events which show the written tradition to be found wanting (Friesen, 1996: xiii-xxvi). To be fair, however, it must be acknowledged that the two traditions are not mutually exclusive, the written having grown out of the oral as a vital part of the natural progression of human civilization.

## The Oral Tradition

A common method of delineating the oral tradition is to conceive of the process as one of verbally handing down stories, beliefs and customs from one generation to the next. While this definition is technically correct, at the surface it glosses over the impact of the oral tradition which in certain circumstances has the same effect as the written word. Among some Plains tribes, when council was called and tobacco was passed among the elders, and or when the pipe was smoked, it was understood by those gathered that only the truth would be told during the proceedings. Similarly, in some tribes when the sweetgrass ceremony was practised it indicated that a cleansing of the mind was the desire of the participants, and the way was prepared for honest and "pure" deliberation. To those not familiar with the ritual, the sweetgrass ceremony consists of making a smudge with sweetgrass in a bowl or other vessel. Prayers are said, and then the bowl is passed from person to person with each individual "scooping" smoke from the bowl and fanning it over the face and the body. The movement much resembles the figurative washing of the face and the body.

The oral tradition was not only a means by which to transmit cultural knowledge to succeeding generations, it was a way of preserving and interpreting truth for a specific time and place, as well as for mediating elaborate ritualistic processes. By participating in ceremonial procedures, powerful religious and moral sensibilities were evoked in the experience of the people. Basic to this context, were root symbolic forms which encoded the fundamental meanings borne in the oral tradition and enacted in the ritual processes (Harrod, 1995: 22f). The fact that the oral tradition did not feature written forms should in no way be construed to suggest that its structures were any less complex nor its spiritual and moral impact any less significant.

One of the major concerns of every ethnocultural or religious community is the transmission of its philosophical beliefs, values and customs to succeeding generations. Basic to most tribal cultural configurations is knowledge related to tribal origins, migrations and spiritual truths. There are concerns about procedures for ensuring that this knowledge is being inculcated by the young, and the procedures include specified rituals and the art of relating stories. Usually these stories are called myths or legends when they emanate from First Nations' sources and historical accounts or parables when they refer to the Bible. In Old Testament times, storytelling was a popular form of conveying truth and this practice did not diminish during the Jewish transition from tribal society to nation. Some of the parables told by Jesus (like that of the Good Samaritan in Luke 10:25-37) are well-known to people who are otherwise quite unfamiliar with the contents of the Bible.

## The Significance of Storytelling

Indian legends have often been singled out as the most conventional means of transmitting Aboriginal cultural values and beliefs, sometimes at the expense of failing to take into account the function of parallel established institutional rituals and symbols. To begin with, Aboriginal legends are unique. They are truly Indian stories, and as such they comprise the oral Aboriginal literature that is drawn from each particular tribal cultural configuration. Indian stories are pictures of First Nations' life drawn by Indian artists, showing the range of daily challenges and blessings from their point of view. Legends deal with religion, the origins of things, the performances of medicine men and women, and the bravery and singleheartedness of warriors (Grinnell, 1962: xiii). They convey a vast range of cultural knowledge, incorporating folkways, values, beliefs, and the fundamental metaphysical presuppositions that determine the very ground of a particular cultural pattern. There are interesting parallels to be drawn between Aboriginal legends, Old Testament stories and the parables of Jesus.

The content and institutional structures of the Aboriginal oral tradition frequently rely on several motifs. Among the Blackfoot, Crows, Cheyennes and Arapahos, for example, four specific motifs are used – solar, astral, animals and plants. In the first two types, the heavenly bodies play a significant role, particularly as sources of transcendental power. Animals often mediate powers to humans that are associated with their unique characteristics – speed, vision, wisdom or cunning. They are also employed in adventuresome and comic tales related for entertainment purposes. Plants play a less dominant role, albeit among the Crows, for example, the cultivation of tobacco is connected to their origin story. For them the ritual of the Tobacco Society is a reenactment of the creation story which renews the people and their world.

Traditionally the oral tradition was well-suited to a fairly conservative human culture that was given only to occasional and relatively minor shifts. No human civilization can function without some element of change, and the oral tradition was appropriately flexible to accommodate this societal need. The written tradition emerged with the invention of the printing press and thereby lent an element of false security to human civilization. The printed page was immediately viewed as constituting a "provable" record, and even a legal foundation by which to affect future developments. Now it was possible to refer to recordings of past happenings without having to consult the elders; history in this sense, "spoke for itself."

Parenthetically, it is useful to keep in mind that while this view is somewhat overstated, so is the belief that the written record is free from interpretations geared to time and place. In addition, the printed page produced some unforeseen side-effects, not all of them necessarily positive. House (1992) contends that the printed page begets nationalism in the capacity that written forms of propaganda influence people to perceive of themselves as belonging to an entity beyond specific geographic limitations. By reading about their broader identity, they could feel part of something more expansive than their local tribe; they could even be stirred to be willing to die for their larger ethnocultural community or nation without even experiencing face-to-face contact with other members of their wider fraternity.

## Types of Legends

The compilation and study of Indian legends is a source of enriched learning for the pursuer of such knowledge forms. In the first instance, legends appear to have been told for a variety of purposes and in at least two specific settings, formal and informal. The latter often took place at the spur of the moment when it appeared appropriate to reprimand or perhaps to entertain someone. Also, sometimes on a winter evening when the people had stretched out to rest for the night a storyteller would begin a tale. Among Crow storytellers, a narrator might expect to get an occasional response from his listeners, failing which he assumed that they had fallen asleep and would stop talking (Lowie, 1963: 137). Formal storytelling was more directly connected to the occasion of deliberate moral or spiritual instruction. Some legends or myths were so sacred as to have their telling restricted to the celebration of an event such as the Sundance. On these occasions, only recognized or designated persons could engage in their telling.

In analyzing the compositions specifically of Plains Indian legends there appear to have been at least four kinds in operation throughout Plains Indian history. Although these stories may be differentiated for the purpose of analysis (a non-Indian habit), there was also considerable overlap in their use. The types include: (i) *legends for amusement,* which were often about the Trickster (sometimes called Napi, Nanabush, Coyote, îktomni, or other names), and related primarily for entertainment; (ii) *teaching legends,* which were employed for the purpose of dispensing historical or cultural information about the tribe; (iii) *moral legends,* which were intended to teach ideal or "right" forms of behavior and perhaps to suggest to the hearer that only certain forms of behavior would be approved; and, (iv) *spiritual legends,* which could be related only by an elder or other approved individual at a certain time and place, perhaps for a price, and were considered forms of worship.

1. Legends for Amusement

*Legends told for amusement* are often highly humorous even to non-Indian listeners, many of them pertaining to actions of the Trickster. In one Blackfoot story, for example, the Trickster is walking along the shore of a lake and he looking for food for he is hungry. Suddenly he spies what he thinks is a large piece of red meat at the bottom of a pool of water. Believing that it is his good fortune to discover that someone has lost their meat, and it is his to take, he decides to dive to the bottom of the lake to retrieve the meat. He fails in his initial attempt because he cannot dive deeply enough. He then ties rocks to his feet in order to sink deeper into the water. Still, to no avail, so he adds more rocks to his load. Finally, on his fourth try, he reaches the bottom of the pool only to return to the surface out of breath and with only a handful of mud in his hands. It is then that he spies a bunch of red cherries hanging on a branch above the water and it becomes clear to him that the meat he had been diving down to reach was merely the reflection of the cherries in the water. Of course there is a lesson in this tale about the Trickster's selfish joy at someone's else's loss, but the tale is basically told to entertain.

Biblical stories were seldom related for entertainment purposes although it is possible that listeners found some of Jesus Christ's ideas humorous. In the Old Testament, the prophet Jotham (Judges 9:7-15) related an amusing story which clearly enunciated his disapproval of the City of Shechem's choice of a king in one named Abimelech. This man was chosen after several others refused to take the position. Jotham's legend pertains to a group of trees going forth to appoint a king among them. Their first choice was the olive tree which is the most important of all fruit trees in the country. The olive declined on grounds that he did not want to give up his position as supplier of oil by which gods and men were honored. The fig tree was also approached but he declined as well on grounds of the importance of the fruit he produces. Next the vine was invited to take the position, but he refused as well on pretty much the same grounds. As a last resort the bramble, a useless, fruitless weed, was asked to be king. The bramble accepted the honor and this choice points out how ludicrous the idea was. After all, trees could take refuge in the shadow of the lowly bramble bush because it had none to give. The bramble was also subject to easily being set on fire and such a happening could destroy even the finest cedars of Lebanon. The moral of the story is that Shechem chose a weak and useless king named Abimelech and history bore this out.

2. Teaching Legends

In the practice of the First Nations *teaching legends* often utilized animal motifs to explain why things are the way they are. For example, in the Ojibway story of creation, the Great Spirit creates two cranes, lowers them to the earth through an opening in the sky, and instructs them to find a suitable place to live. They are assured that when they can identify an appropriate location they will be turned in a man and a woman and head up a new nation. The two cranes spend a lot of time looking for the right place; they want to make sure that there will be an ample supply of good-tasting and nutritious food. First, they fly over the Great Plains and taste the buffalo, then they take to the forests and taste the deer, the elk and other animals of the forest. After flying over the Great Lakes, they taste the various kinds of fish and decide that this is where they want to live. Their final decision is: "Here is food forever; here we will make our home" (Coffer, 1978: 77). Then the two cranes are turned into humans and become the first parents of the Ojibway Nation.

In some Indian tribes, origin myths particularly were considered property and thus their transmission from generation to generation was carefully safe-guarded. Select individuals would learn a legend by careful listening; then, on mastering the story, would pass it on to succeeding generations, perhaps changing aspects of the story to suit their own tastes. The amendments would center on a different choice of animals or sites referred to in the story and pre-ferred by the teller.

Most parables recorded in the Bible, though they may contain some ele-ments of cultural or historical lore, also have a lesson to teach. The parable of the workers in the vineyard (Matthew 20:1-16), for example, tells us a great deal about land ownership, responsibilities of laborers, and equity of pay. It seems that some workers were hired in the early morning and they worked all day, others were hired on in the afternoon, and some at the very last hour before closing time. When the day was over, they discovered that they had all received the same amount of pay. When the laborers who had worked all day complained to the landlord, he replied, "Don't I have the right to do what I want with my own money? Or are you envious because I am generous?" (Matthew 20:15).

Some commentators suggest that this parable has reference to the com-plaints of the Jews when they discovered that the Johnny-come-lately Gentiles were also invited to participate in the kingdom of God as full heirs. Others sug-gest that the story simply has reference to the fact that God awards redemption to all who call on His name – whenever they call. The reward is the same; they are now children of God and entitled to their just and heavenly rewards.

3. Moral Legends

The plots of *moral legends* convey appropriate and "right" behavior to the listener. Most of Jesus' parables are of this nature albeit some of them might also be interpreted as conveying spiritual truths. A popular moral legend among West Coast Indians is the story of a brave young man whose girlfriend is not particularly impressed with his countenance. She sends him on various missions designed to improve his looks; he is to scrub his face with cedar branches, then with thorns, and so on. On his way to obey the last irrational request, the man has a vision about a woman who can change faces. He finds the woman and she asks him a riddle: "What answers when you call, but can-not speak?" He responds, "Your heart answers when you call but cannot speak." His answer is correct and he is invited to select a face that suits him. He tries to do so, but without success and determines to be happy with what nature has assigned him. Unbeknownst to him, the woman then enhances his appearance. On his way back to camp he is attacked by a large bear, and defeats the creature after a ferocious fight. Suddenly, the bear turns into a beautiful woman who was under a spell which the brave man broke. She offers to serve the man in any way she can, but he extends an invitation of marriage to her instead.

On his arrival back at camp, the young man's friends welcome his new partner and make complimentary comments on his enhanced appearance. His old girlfriend shows up and demands to know who the new woman is and how the man's face got changed. After some coaxing he tells her about the woman who can change faces and she goes off to pursue the old woman. The old woman asks the girlfriend the same riddle, "What answers when you call, but cannot speak," which she answers incorrectly. Her answer is, "a dog," but the correct answer is "your heart." The girlfriend then demands a new face and the old woman says she has the perfect face for her. When the girl looks at the reflection of her new face in a pool of water she screams in dismay. It is the face of one who is cruel, selfish and critical of others. The lesson is obvious, "Pride goes before destruction, a haughty spirit before a fall" (Proverbs 16:18).

Many parables told by Jesus Christ teach lessons about values. The parable of the rich fool (Luke 12:16-21), for example, suggests that life consists of more than riches, the parable of the pharisee and the publican (Luke 18:9-14), teaches that humility is favored above pride by the Almighty, and the parable of the two sons teaches that obedience is better than status (Matthew 21:28-32). Finally, the parable of the ten talents (Matthew 25:14-30) elaborates the principle that one ought to use the gifts given to him or her by the Creator. On a secondary note this parable might also have a political application in the sense of passing along spiritual responsibilities and blessings from Jews to Gentiles.

New Testament parables with a spiritual impact usually pertain to the Kingdom of God and how one may enter it. These parables (see Matthew 13), emphasize that anyone who believes can enter the Kingdom of God, regardless of race, creed or color, and they will be welcomed. They also stress the fact that God is not willing that anyone should perish and so goes out to try to bring everyone into the kingdom. This is illustrated by the parable of the net and the parable of the hidden treasure and the pearl. Reaction to this invitation is shown in the parable of the sower and represented by the different kinds of soil on which the message lands.

4. Spiritual Legends

To discuss *spiritually impacting legends* of the Aboriginal peoples involves an element of uncertainty about possession of property (legends are considered property), as well as appropriateness. For these reasons, this tradition will be honored here and no spiritually-related legend will be related nor summarized. It is important to know that probing into the content of sacred legends is a very sensitive and restricted activity. Traditionally, some legends could only be told at a certain time of year. The Shoshonis, for example, would not tell old legends during the "snowy months," the Crows would not tell them during the summer, and the Blackfeet would not relate them while it was still light (Clark, 1988: 15).

In one southwest tribe the services of an Elder had to be requested four days before the scheduled delivery of a spiritual legend. The elder, in this case, prepared for the event by fasting and offering tobacco. Further, the legend could not simply be told at any time; the official period, when no payment was required, was the four days of winter solstice, "when the sun stands still." Other winter nights were permitted if the hearers would pay to hear the legend. Under no circumstances, however, could the legend nor even any part of it be told in the summer (Underhill, 1965: 31-32).

A tribe's origin belief or story was central to the entire religious system of most traditional tribes, and often premised on these assumptions: (i) everything in the universe, including people, has spiritual power, or life force; (ii) all spiritual forces are interconnected; and, (iii) humankind has a responsibility to that interconnection. The earth, which is the basis for such connections and which provides life to all, is sacred (Josephy, 1989: 79). Thus legend-telling comprised the activity of theological instruction at its most significant level.

Legends made up only one component of a tribe's spiritual repertoire which also included ceremonies, rituals, songs and dances. These were represented or supplemented by physical objects such as fetishes, pipes, painted designs, medicine bundles and shrines of sorts. Familiarity with these components comprised religious knowledge, and everything learned was committed to memory. Viewed together these entries represented spiritual connections between people and the universe which, with appropriate care, resulted in a lifestyle of assured food supply, physical well-being and the satisfying of the needs and wants of the society and its members.

The structure of Indian legends follows a unique format and procedure and there is a great deal of overlap among legends of varying tribes. Often two stories in the same tribe might have the same beginning and then the versions would digress. The stories could even be told in almost identical language for a few paragraphs and then veer off in a direction to suit the narrator. The digression was designed to accommodate the style of the narrators who had the liberty to depict their personal every-day life experiences in their own style. This approach also allowed the teller to adapt the story to the perceived needs and interests of the listeners.

## The Transition from Oral to Written Tradition

Adherents to the written tradition are often unaware of the evolution of this mode of communication, particularly in terms of esteemed works of truth. Although it may be a delicate subject to pursue, the development of sacred writings such as the Bible is illustrative of the tendency of believers to confirm the efficacy of these works without necessarily examining how they were derived. Let the "written" record show that this discussion is not in any way intended to demean either the efficacy of the Bible nor the revered place in occupies in Christendom.

Many Christians are taught to believe that the Bible is an amazing collection of sixty-six smaller volumes penned by a myriad of forty different writers spanning forty generations and a 1 500 year history. The catalog of writers includes twenty occupations such as a political leader, a fisherman, a military general, a physician, a king and a tax collector. Its subject matter includes hundreds of controversial subjects which, when they are studied, often create opposing opinions (Keck, 1978: 17-18). Still it is claimed that though the various books of the Bible were written on three different continents, and in three different languages, this does not change its inherent unity (McDowell, 1986: 16).

It cannot be denied that the Bible constitutes great literature with one of its alluring features being the penetrating discussions it stimulates about philosophy and morals (Herr, 1982: 27). Its contents cover every conceivable subject expressed in all literary forms, including prose, poetry, romance, mystery, biography, science and history (Hall, 1990: 7). It has inspired some of the noblest art forms and the loftiest music. Few creators of the arts have ever captured a high level of drama and poetry without understanding the Bible. Its laws furnish much of the background for the legal systems of western civilization (Hubbard, 1971: 17).

Against this volume of high praise and awe it is perhaps a bit daring to remind Biblical adherents that their package of sacred writings gradually emerged from an oral tradition. The weakest link in the chain of growth is manifest in a study of the available manuscripts which made it into the canon and those which were rejected. Evidently there was quite a collection of works available which had endured through the oral-to-written evolution and the compilers faced a very difficult task. Even when a first canon list was concocted it failed to gain uniform acceptance by many religious authorities for many decades. Finally, perhaps based singularly on the criterion of endurance, the Bible's present format grew to be accepted. Even then it should be mentioned that the Roman Catholic canon contains several more books than the Protestant version.

The Bible is essentially a history of the Jewish nation who from the time of its patriarch, Abraham, wandered nomadically across the eastern desert. Like other peoples of the oral tradition the First Nations carried their library of truths in their heads. They developed amazing retentive abilities and their storytellers put the saga of their ancestors into poetic form which was easy to remember. For the first five hundred years of their existence the Israelites passed along their traditions by word of mouth, sharing their history by repeat-ing the same ideas and phrases, generation after generation.

When the Jewish kingdom became a settled reality at the time of King David and his successor, Solomon, a literature of sorts simultaneously began to develop. The Book of the Song of Solomon, reported in Judges chapter five, is considered one of the oldest pieces and may be dated to about 1125 B.C. The Song of Miriam, contained in the Book of Exodus, dates from around 1280 B.C. (Kodell, 1985: 26).

Although the canonization of the Old Testament took place over many generations, by comparison, the New Testament was collated over a relatively short period of time. First references to the New Testament as a standard for faith and practice appeared as early as A.D. 200 in the writings of Clement of Rome and Ignatius of Antioch. As the canon was being formed several newer religious writings appeared which were eventually rejected as part of the canon. The Epistle of Barnabas and the Shepherd of Hermas (an allegory by a Roman Christian) appeared to be the most popular. Around A.D. 170, the Muratorian Document (named for the discoverer), enunciated that the Shepherd of Hermas could be read in Christian circles, but it was not to be considered part of the canon.

When the canon fathers met to finalize the editing of the Bible they uti-lized a variety of factors in determining which manuscripts should be includ-ed. First, there was the challenge of identifying *official* manuscripts, and this was a perplexing problem since there were so many editions to choose from. Thus the procedure became one of studying the manuscripts and working out the basic theory and establishing the criteria by which the true text would be determined. The next task was to determine how these criteria and theory would regulate the basic text of any given passage (Ramm, 1987: 93f). On this foundation the canon fathers also decided to consider the apostolic origins of each manuscript, the importance of the community which it addressed, and the centrality of the doctrine it contained. Even then, according to contemporary evangelical scholars, in the final analysis, it was the church's awareness, under the guidance of the Holy Spirit (Great Spirit), that certain manuscripts were considered authentic (Kodell, 1985: 39).

Historical criticism has revealed that the exact origins of many parts of the Bible are quite obscure. For example, the name of the prophet whose work is contained in Isaiah chapters 40-55 has been forgotten since the time when these materials were added to the Book of Isaiah. Similarly, no one remem-bers who complied the manuscript "Q" which contained the sayings of Jesus and which the Gospel writers quoted in Matthew and Luke. Besides, no one knows who wrote the Book of the Hebrews although authorship is sometimes attributed to the first century church missionary, the Apostle Paul. It is clear that memory was more pious than accurate in attributing the Pentateuch to

Moses, the Psalms to David and the Book of Proverbs to Solomon, or in holding that both Matthew and John actually wrote the Gospels attributed to their names (Keck, 1978: 69f).

Coupled with the question of the canon is the matter of scriptural interpretation. Over the centuries a number of historical schools of thought have emerged, each of which has stressed any of the following themes in scriptural interpretation – allegory, literalism, hermeneutics or neo-orthodoxy. Philo, a Jewish proponent of allegory, warned that a passage of scripture was to be allegorically interpreted if: (i) a statement says anything unworthy of God; (ii) if a statement is contradictory with some other statement or in any other way presents the interpreter with a difficulty; or, (iii) if the record itself is allegorical in nature (Ramm, 1987: 221f).

By the third century, after the Jews had made an official declaration of their Old Testament canon, the Christian church was still unaware that the Jews had a shorter canon. St. Ananasius, who was instructed by Jewish teachers, made a strong appeal for the acceptance of the shorter canon by the Christian church. St. Jerome translated the Bible into Latin and also pled for the shorter canon but was not able to realize his preference. Thus until the time of the Reformation in the sixteenth century, Jerome's Latin Vulgate, which contained the longer version, was the standard Christian Bible. Despite the objections of Martin Luther to some books in the canon, in 1546, the Council of Trent declared that the longer Old Testament was to be the official canon. This collection is currently accepted by all three streams of the Christian tradition today, Roman Catholic, Greek Orthodox and Protestant. The Catholic version also contains several additional ancient Jewish books known as the "Apocrypha"; however, neither Protestants nor Catholics consider these works to be divinely-inspired.

Bible-believing Christians will argue that in the final analysis it is not a matter of how the canon was edited nor the exactitude of its interpretation. If the Bible has prevailed all these centuries, despite many attacks and criticisms, it must have validity. When American evangelist, Billy Graham, was asked about his position on the canon he simply replied that he had decided one day to accept and preach the Bible as though it was God's truth. He stated that he left questions of authenticity to the scholars and he had ample reason to believe that, since the day of his decision to accept the whole Bible as God's word, his decision had been the right one. Undoubtedly Graham would be joined in this claim by other Bible-believing Christians. A text that this group might wish to employ to undergird their stance could be: "All Scripture is God-breathed and is useful for teaching, rebuking, correcting and training in righteousness, so that the man of God may be thoroughly equipped for every good work" (II Timothy 3:16,17).

For Bible believers of a conservative persuasion there are several criteria that determine a credible interpretation of the Holy Book. Without these qualifications no valid interpretation can be made and the Bible will merely comprise another piece of literature. The qualifications for correct and meaningful interpretation include: (i) interpreters must be "born again"; (ii) they must have a passion to know God's word; (iii) they must have a deep reverence for God; and, (iv) they must have complete dependence upon the Holy Spirit to guide and direct them (Ramm, 1987: 13).

## Conclusion

The fact that the written word originated from within the oral tradition does not in any way validate the former as a reliable body of truth. It does, however, show the natural link between the two traditions and underscores the fact that the two forms of knowledge transmission are really part and parcel of a connected phenomenon. Cultures that have traditionally relied on the oral tradition by definition convey no recognized, stationary body of literature to transmit or to build upon. Knowledge is, after all, a "living" phenomenon, and like other cultural forms, cannot be frozen in time. This is particularly true in Native cultures where the role of elders continues to be significant (Couture, 1991a).

The traditional Aboriginal world yet untouched by European immigration, like other tribal societies, placed a great deal of reliance on implicit forms of institutional structure which were perpetuated by practice. From a tribal viewpoint, theological truths consisted of more than legal doctrines or statements of belief. The traditional Aboriginal lifestyle valued "being" instead of "doing," and "doing" instead of "talking about what could or should be done." This perspective was very much dependent upon the continuation and strengthening of tribal practices through the oral tradition. In this context, "the letter killeth, but the spirit giveth life." While this approach has been quite appropriate to and proven reliable in the "old world" of pre-European contact, it has not fared so well in the world of the microchip. It remains to be seen what will happen in the First Nation world of the third millennium if the modern penchant for mass-produced discs of stored verbiage is allowed to replace the Indian tradition of regarding life as a continual process of sacred trust.

# Eight

## Theological Comparisons and Contrasts:
## Soteriology, Deontology and Eschatology

It is universally recognized that all human societies, prehistoric and contemporary, have in place a stipulated means by which their members can gain
Divine approval. There may not be consensus on the exact nature of supernatural manifestations, but all are pretty well agreed that humankind has an obligation to the Supernatural and must depend on Divine approval for everything
from daily sustenance to the hereafter. In traditional Plains Ojibway theology,
for example, it was believed that the Manitous ordered the people to keep certain ceremonies, and if they failed to do so, their crops would fail. At one point
they neglected to hold the Sundance for period of seven years during which
time no rain fell. When they reestablished the ceremony, the crops were again
watered by the Almighty (Pettipas, 1994: 185).

By now it will be evident that the basic premise of this book is that there
is a great deal of similarity between the Old Testament perspective and that of
the Indigenous Peoples of North America in the precontact period. Since the
New Testament Christian tradition builds on its Jewish roots, the degree of
similarity with its theological forebearers is also substantial. In light of these
similarities and connections the context of the three doctrines discussed here
pertain specifically to precontact First Nations, Old Testament Israel and conservative New Testament Christianity.

## Soteriology

According to the Christian tradition, the salvation of humankind is entirely in the hands of the just God who is at the same time merciful and long suffering. It is because of the latter attributes that despite the fall of humankind
God has made an arrangement whereby the people He has created can regain
His favor. The singular requirement is simple; "And everyone who calls on the
name of the Lord will be saved" (Acts 2:21). The Christian God is a God of
grace; He, by His own choice, awards unmerited favor to humankind even
though He demands that people try to live up to His moral laws. Being human,

they will fail, of course, and this is known and expected by the infinite God. This is where grace comes in. Because man has a bent to sin and to fail, he has little choice but to realize that unmerited favor is the only means by which salvation can be realized;

> For by grace are ye saved through faith; and that not of yourselves; it is the gift of God; Not of works, lest any man should boast. For we are his workmanship, created in Christ Jesus unto good works, which God hath before ordained that we should walk in them. (Ephesians 2:8-10 KJV)

Logically, one would expect that the unworthy recipients of unmerited favor would be happy to spend their lives serving the One who made salvation possible for them. This too, must have been in God's plan when He urged believers through the Apostle, St. Paul, "For we are God's workmanship, created in Christ Jesus to do good works, which God has prepared in advance for us to do" (Ephesians 2:10). The Book of James affirms this principle;

> What good is it, my brothers, if a man claims to have faith but has no deeds? Can such faith save him? . . . In the same way, faith by itself, if it is not accompanied by action, is dead. (James 2:14, 17)

Contemporary theologians concur with James that faith without works is dead, and many of them have wrestled for generations with the question as to whether the same truth is taught by St. Paul when he raises the issue;

> What then shall we say that Abraham, our forefather, discovered in this matter? If, in fact, Abraham was justified by works, he had something to boast about – but not before God. What does the Scripture say? "Abraham *believed* God and it was credited to him as righteousness." (Romans 4:1-3, italics mine)

A way for theologians to resolve this apparent controversy has been to point out that Paul believed that individuals are justified by faith, not by works. However, as James states, logically and naturally works should follow after one manifests personal faith.

A study of the doctrine of salvation in Aboriginal theology takes the scholar in a slightly different direction. To begin with, Chief John Snow of the Nakoda Sioux describes the first meeting of Stoney Indians and missionaries;

> The concept of God was nothing new to us. The only thing that was different was the terminology. We call our God *Wakâ Tâga*, the Great Spirit. . . . So there were questions about the new religion, but it sounded good and its basic teachings were not unfamiliar. Besides, we did not have disputes regarding religion. There were some disputes over hunting grounds and fishing areas, but not religion! We were aware of the diversity of forms of worship among the various tribes, but the Supreme Being was the Great Spirit. We have been taught not to question various forms or ways of worshipping the Creator. Who were we to question? (Snow, 1977: 17)

Chief Snow goes on to suggest that there were no atheists in traditional Plains Indian culture. From childhood on, youngsters were taught to honor, and respect the Great Spirit and to thank Him daily for His many gifts. There was never a question about believing in God and trying to serve Him.

This was a given in First Nations' culture and children were taught their faith from the time of birth. They were then raised in the faith of the family and given opportunity to affirm their faith on reaching adulthood. Respect and obeisance to the Creator were reinforced through rituals and ceremonies and individual and group prayers – lots of prayers. As Chief Tecumseh of the Shawnee Nation put it,

> When you arise in the morning, give thanks for the light, Give thanks for the morning, for your life and strength. Give thanks for your food and the joy of living. If you see no reason for giving thanks, rest assured, the fault lies within yourself. (Friesen, 1998: 14)

Promoters of the Christian doctrine of eternal security will find little consolation in Aboriginal theology, for Native spiritual leaders interpreted the relationship of humans to God as one of continuous entreatment with humankind always seeking to Divine approval and guidance. It was never the case that anyone could say with assurance that they had reached the state where the Creator was permanently pleased with their behavior. The spiritual leaders of the First Nations saw each individual as being on a personal journey of spiritual growth in which they continually sought Divine approval. The nature of this journey was designated by the Creator and highly personal. Individuals could consult with elders and offer prayers and obtain assistance to determine the course of that journey, but the nature of fulfilment of the Divine mandate was individualistic and gradual. As Bear Heart (1998: 245) put it, "Finding yourself, looking within, is the most important thing in life. 'This is where I stand. This is who I am.'" The Ojibway had a saying, "No man begins to be until he has seen his vision" (Johnston, 1988: 119). By this they meant that humans were viewed as spontaneous beings made out of nothing, but endowed with the capacity for vision – much like their Creator. Each individual was to seek and fulfil that vision and do so along moral lines. Human's life obligations were to be regarded in a moral sense.

Each human act was to reflect the connection of the individual to the Creator through the vision. The process of salvation, therefore, was regarded as just that – a process, rather than a state of being. St. Paul's admonition to the Philippian church captures this stance when he states, "Therefore, my dear friends, as you have always obeyed – not only in my presence, but now much more in my absence continue to work out your salvation with fear and trembling" (Philippians 2:12). The question of good works never came up in Aboriginal culture because, as we shall see in the next section on deontology, it was inherent in their cultural and spiritual system and considered to be part and parcel of daily living.

The concept of the Trinity is not identifiable in First Nations' theology, although they did perceive of a middle range of spiritual beings or helpers somewhere between the earth and the clouds. These spirits were willing to extend assistance to earthlings and did so on the basis of prayers and spiritual songs. Also called "grandfathers" by the Sioux, the spirits, along with those of animals, birds, insects and the like could be called on by sacred persons to enable the people to live respectable lives. The grandfathers could assist with cures and help with other maladies and their wisdom could be passed down from one generation to the next with great care (Powers, 1977: 200). The fact that First Nations recognized the moving of the Spirit or spirits as an active force in their lives parallels the notion of the Spirit of God as a Divine helper in the Christian life. Both traditions, Aboriginal and Christian, foster the concept that the Creator originally made an arrangement whereby His created beings could be guided and succoured in time of need. In this context, the Old Testament's undefined version of the moving of the Spirit of God (Genesis 1:1) is closer to that of the Aboriginal version than that of Christian theology.

Perhaps the most difficult concept to contrast is the New Testament notion promulgated by conservative Christianity that salvation can be attained only in the name of Jesus Christ (Acts 4:12). In an intriguing discussion, Osage theologian Tinker (1998: 143f) points out that this approach is problematic because the Greek word, "saved" is identical to the word, "healed." In Acts 4:9, the disciples, Peter and John, are questioned as to the basis on which a man was healed by their ministry. They reply that he was healed (saved) in the name of Jesus Christ. The word used means "to heal," which is the same word used in Acts 4:12 which applies to "being saved" or obtaining salvation. Tinker suggests that both healing and salvation come through God and God alone. According to Tinker, the name Jesus is synonymous with the Old Testament name Joshua and is a shortened version of the Hebrew word for God, Yahweh. The name Jesus means God saves or God heals. The name Jesus itself was commonly used in biblical times and of itself did not ascribe any specific power to Jesus Christ. As Tinker states:

> I want to suggest that this verse, typically used by Amer-European missionaries to coerce our conversion to Christianity, has been consistently misread and misinterpreted in the missionary claims of Christian exclusivity and superiority. Commentators consistently miss the most obvious point of the story; namely, that the reader is supposed to know a bit more about the name of Jesus and to draw out the meaning of the story from the meaning of the name. (Tinker, 1996: 145)

If Tinker's analysis has merit, the theological gates are opened to the study of alternative cultural interpretations and nomenclature to describe God's saving power. The difficulty that is not explained away is the interpretation of texts that command procedure to salvation through God's Son, Jesus Christ, that is, John 3:16, "For God so loved the world that he gave his one and only

Son that whoever believes in him shall not perish but have eternal life." Acts 16:31 poses a similar scenario, "Believe in the Lord Jesus, and you will be saved – you and your household." The apostle, John, is even clearer at the end of his discussion of salvation when he states that God has placed everything in the hands of His Son. "Whoever believes in the Son has eternal life but whoever rejects the Son, will not see life, for God's wrath remains on him" (John 3:36).

A reconciliation of the two theological perspectives is probably not possible in this brief a space, but the extent of parallels noted should motivate the serious scholar to further examination of both views. Had this outlook been adopted at the time of first contact it is possible that a great deal of today's misunderstanding could have been avoided.

## Deontology

Sociologists who study religion point out that a religious tradition has at least three elements, each handed down and developed in the multitude of ways that traditions are passed on. The first element is the formulation of a mythical or philosophical cosmology to define the rudimentary structures and limits of the world. This set of postulations will explain the fundamental structures and limits of the universe and calculate the basic ways of explaining how things are and what they mean.

The second element of religion requires that such a tradition have some conception of and practical procedures for fundamental transformation aimed at relating persons harmoniously with the universe – a path of spiritual regeneration or perfection. As we have discussed, in theistic religions, particularly Christianity, this usually means salvation or "getting right with God." The Aboriginal peoples opted for a more continuous rather than instantaneous interpretation of this concept.

The third essential element to defining religion pertains to ceremonies and rituals. Rituals comprise a finite set of repeatable and symbolic actions that epitomize the things a tradition treats as crucial to defining the normative human place in the cosmos. Early layers of ritual epitomize the hunt, nurturing of agricultural fertility, acknowledgement of political authority and acts of commitment to other individuals (Friesen, 1995b: 77). A study of deontological considerations in tribal societies will reveal a great deal of emphasis on the oral tradition, storytelling and the enactment of ceremonies and rituals. This implies that the First Nations of North America were very concerned about passing on these traditions to succeeding generations.

Most Indigenous Peoples of North America had in place a governing system based on one of two varying models. Either they adhered to a hereditary model whereby chiefs and principal leaders followed their parents into such roles, or they adhered to the basic structure of the clan system. In the latter paradigm, appointments of chiefs and council were made by individuals (often men or woman) on the basis of their position on the clan. Neither of these models of social and/or religious structure was exclusive for there were variations based on need. War chiefs and hunting chiefs, for example, were selected for specific missions in either format. There were instances of apprenticeship whereby young men became students of respected spiritual leaders and trained to fulfil their roles as successors. Finally, there were also instances when individuals were assigned special roles based on manifested powers or gifts that might have become theirs based on particular visions.

Although the dominant spiritual tones for a tribe were set by the shamans, priests or medicine men and women, in traditional Indigenous cultures children were principally taught the moral rudiments of living by their grandparents and other relatives. The role of parents was supplementary to the process since grandparents and elders were viewed as having a much better grasp of the living ways. Like the Old Testament Hebrews, First Nations took seriously the challenge of indoctrinating their children. They adhered to a code similar to the one outlined by Moses in the Book of Deuteronomy:

> These commandments that I give you today are to be upon your hearts. Impress them on your children. Talk about them when you sit at home and when you walk along the road, when you lie down and when you get up. Tie them as symbols on your hands and bind them on your foreheads. Write them on the doorframes of your houses and on your gates. (Deuteronomy 6:6-9)

In the New Testament, Christ is seen as supportive of the strong Old Testament mandate towards loving children and protecting them from possible harm. These tendencies are evident from two scripture passages in the Gospel of Matthew. In the first instance Jesus is asked by His disciples who would be the greatest in the kingdom of heaven. Jesus responds by calling a child to the gathering and making the statement,

> I tell you the truth, unless you change and become like little children, you will never enter the kingdom of heaven. Therefore, whoever humbles himself like this child is the greatest in the kingdom of heaven." (Matthew 18:3-4)

Jesus goes on to say that no one should ever harm a child. It would be better for anyone who does choose to harm a child to have a millstone hung around his neck and he be drowned in the depths of the sea (Matthew 18:6). Quite possibly, the First Nations of long ago would have agreed with this clear statement on child-raising.

The second instance in which Jesus showed particular interest in children occurred when a group of mothers tried to approach Jesus that He might bless their children. The disciples, thinking that Jesus could not be bothered with little ones, turned their mothers away. When Jesus became aware of this, he became quite agitated and severely rebuked his disciples. Then He took the children in his arms, placed his hands on them, and blessed them with another reminder; "Jesus said, 'Let the little children come to me, and do not hinder them, for the kingdom of heaven belongs to such as these'" (Matthew 19:14).

McFee (1972: 96f), in an investigation of Indian values, enunciated five specific values of traditional Blackfeet culture which once framed the foundations of their spiritual life: individualism, bravery, skill, wisdom and generosity. Zeilinger (1997: 56f), working with the Sioux, discovered four foundational values: generosity, courage (or bravery), respect and wisdom. McFee's study highlighted major value cores that remain highly acclaimed among the Blackfeet today even though their interpretation has changed somewhat. Skill, for example, used to apply principally to hunting and warfare, but now has been transferred to dancing, singing, arts, crafts and oratorical skills. Individualism today, as in traditional times, applies to community status, name and self-image, even though the means by which to attain these have been altered somewhat in recent times.

It would probably be fair to say that the four principal pillars of traditional Indian tribal societies would have been respect, generosity, individualism and wisdom. Respect is closely related to honor in the sense that one regards everything, the earth, all living things such as plants and animals and people as having a dignity of their own. In order for people to live together they have to respect one another. The old are respected for their wisdom and the young for the fact that they will be responsible for maintaining the identity of the tribe. To an extent the traditional notion of respect is slowly returning, particularly with regard to the resurrection of the importance of the role of elder (Medicine, 1987; Couture, 1991b). Bear Heart (1998: 19), representing the viewpoint of the Muskogee Creek Indians, states that "When you have respect for the elders, it extends to everything else, including all of nature and its life forms." Chief John Snow of the Stoney Nation echoes this sentiment;

> Old people were a very important part of tribal society. They were the wise elders with a lifetime of experience that was valued by all. They taught our children, tutored our youth, and advised younger adults and tribal councils. (Snow, 1977: 5)

Norma Kassi (1996: 74) of the Gwich'in Nation notes that she was brought up living entirely on the land and she was taught to respect and love everything. Her grandparents even taught her that walking on Mother Earth had to be done showing great respect. Even today, the elders of the Gwich'in Nation caution the youth to be very strong, but not become militant. They advise that the longer one walks with respect, performs acts of kindness, and reveres one's ancestors and the teachings of Mother Earth, the better the ultimate outcome. The struggle to regain respect for the earth is a universal concern and, unfortunately, it will probably be regarded as a serious concern only when too much damage to the environment has been done.

Generosity among tribal cultures always applied first of all to immediate family, then to all of one's relatives and even to strangers who came to visit. The Old Testament Hebrews were warned by the Creator that they should be kind to strangers because they themselves were once in a similar situation, that is, "Thou shalt neither vex a stranger, nor oppress him; for ye were strangers in the land of Egypt" (Exodus 22:21 KJV). Human relationships were seen to be the arena in which people gave evidence of their spirituality. As an Ojibway elder informed Rupert Ross (1996: 146),

> According to our traditional thought, if we fail to organize all aspects of our lives, including our work, around making positive – or – healing contributions to our relationships, then we are actually making negative contributions instead.

Kindness was not only viewed as its own reward in traditional Indian country, people were looked up to on the basis of being able to look after their families as well as sharing with others. To be called a "stingy person" would be the greatest insult anyone could receive. Giveaway dances were basically sponsored to impress upon others the extent to which one could be generous. The Sioux phrase "and all my relations" extended the obligation of caring and sharing beyond the human pale to all living things.

When the Spanish explorer, Christopher Columbus, first met the Aboriginal Peoples he was most impressed with their generosity.

> They are so ingenuous and free with all they have, that no one would believe it who has not seen it; of anything that they possess, if it be asked of them, they never say no; on the contrary, they invite you to share it and show as much love as if their hearts went with it, and they are content with whatever trifle be given them, whether it be a thing of value or of petty worth. (McPherson, 1998: 79-80)

A Jesuit priest, Father Le Jeune, who worked among the Hurons made quite positive observations about Native generosity, similar to those made by Columbus. One notation he made of the Indians, describes their "shining noble moral virtues, their generous exchange of gifts and their hospitality towards all strangers" (McPherson, 1998: 80).

The flip side of generosity was that family members could expect an individual with resources to lend assistance to others whenever there was need. This meant that a person of means was fair game to those who lacked anything. The needy could ask for assistance if they were overlooked by mistake or if the holder of means was not aware of their plight, or they could simply avail themselves of whatever they desired. Resources were seen as belonging to the family, the clan or the camp, and the "owner" was viewed as a temporary custodian. Thus sharing in the contemporary sense would be a misnomer. The traditional view was that those who have, had better share!

One of the reasons fur traders and missionaries had so much impact in Native tribal societies was because they were so warmly welcomed into the midst of the resident peoples. The newcomers were fed, listened to and made to feel at home in every way. When the visitors declared that they were "Men of God" the Indians listened carefully because it was their belief that if someone made such a claim he or she should be given an audience. It was tradition that if anyone made a claim about having had Divine contact in some form, usually through a vision, that person deserved an opportunity to share it. Sadly, as the Aboriginals listened to the missionaries they received a teaching for which they were not prepared. It was about resources and land ownership. As Chief John Snow notes, "Before the whiteman came, we had the land and they had the Bible. Now, we have the Bible and they have the land" (Snow, 1977: 16).

McFee (1972: 96) elaborates the dimensions of individualism among the Blackfeet in terms of individual achievement, social acceptance, increased prestige and higher status, but the nature of each of these was to be determined by the individual. The evidence for this may be drawn from traditional child-raising habits. No one ever forced a child to do anything. Children were respected and allowed to live their way into personally-determined patterns. Personal choice was maximized. Children were wanted, loved and cared for, but not coddled. A mother might have suggested to a child that he or she share a toy with a sibling or friend, but the matter would be dropped if the child was persistent in refusing to do so. A child running around the room where an important meeting was going on would never be reprimanded even though the noise would make hearing difficult. The spiritual implication of this approach underscores the belief that every individual, starting with early childhood, was on a personal spiritual journey and the nature of that course was not be interfered with by anyone.

The biblical record substantiates this frame of mind in the many recorded instances of in which individuals received personal mandates from God to fulfil certain tasks. For example, the call of Moses (Exodus 3), Samuel (I Samuel 3), Amos (Amos 7:14-16), and Saul, who later became Paul (Acts 9).

The First Nations considered the knowledge and wisdom of the old people as very important to the well-being of their people. Wisdom was interpreted as respecting the Creator and the world He provided, being humble and caring for others. Suzuki (1992: 9) states that the Native mind is embodied in the traditional ecstatic healer or shaman, and this tradition is as old as humankind itself. Its taproot descends down deep into the rich Pleistocene soil of an ancient hunting-gathering way of life, and its tender leaves still unfurl to this day. Native wisdom, with its various incarnations and constant modifications, helped people navigate through countless crucial cultural transitions ranging from the domestication of animals and early agriculture to the margins of modern industrialization.

The First Nations considered knowledge sacred because it had been handed down for many generations and as such comprised a valued source of understanding the forces of nature. Elder Frank Fools Crow stated,

> The power and ways are given to us to be passed on to others. To think or do anything else is pure selfishness. We only keep them and get more by giving them away, and if we do not give them away we lose them. (McGaa, 1995: 158)

When the younger generations were being taught the old ways they were instructed to listen carefully to what was being taught. Beck, Walters and Francisco (1990: 48) postulate that "In order that knowledge did not get separated from experience, wisdom from divinity, the elders stressed listening and waiting, not asking why." Elders today lament that metaphysics and extraordinary ways of learning have virtually disappeared from daily life and the educational systems of western civilization. They worry that this trend is dangerous and ultimately weakens the individual and the community. Unless interest in studying traditional Aboriginal wisdom is revived there is little hope for finding alternative ways to be good stewards of the universe.

Traditionally the Indigenous Peoples did not separate the search for knowledge from sacred learning or what we now call religious education. The wisdom of the elders included the whole parameters of human experience including the Divine connection. Sensitivity towards learning from any and all experiences – spiritual, social, personal or physical – opened up to the people elements of knowledge of the Great Mysteries which were considered the only way to comprehend even rudimentary aspects of the intangible laws of the universe. In the words of the Psalmist, "Open my eyes that I may see wonderful things in your law" (Psalm 119:18).

## Eschatology

Eschatology is the division of theology that deals with last things; its principal concerns have to do with the destiny of the individual and that of the universe. Fitzwater (1953: 517) suggests that eschatology is inevitable since virtually every civilization known to humankind has formulated conceptualizations pertaining to the future life. It is characteristic of rational humans to ask questions such as, "Does death end it all? Do individuals at death enter another form of existence? Are conditions in the future state better or worse than in this life?"

Many formulated eschatological theories pertaining to Christianity are generalized or vague, but they exist as a devised means of comfort for those who remain behind when loved ones die. They are principally intended to foster the ideal of tribal perpetuation beyond human existence. The Old

Testament contains numerous references to a grand and glorious day when all nations shall worship the God of Israel (Psalm 86:9, Isaiah 2:4, Ezekiel 39:8, Hosea 2:18). Several passages speak to the nature of the intermediate state (Psalm 17:15, Proverbs 15:24, Isaiah 5:14), implying that the dead cannot be returned to the earth although the soul is conscious after death (Matthew 17:3-4, Luke 9:32-33). The New Testament picks up on this in Christ's parable of the rich fool (Luke 12:19-31). The rich man has great plans to grow more grain and build huge barns in which to store it. That night God demands the man's soul; he perishes and so lays waste to his pompous bragging. The lesson is simple, Do not lay up treasures for yourself on earth, "For where your treasure is, there will your heart be also" (Luke 12:34 KJV).

The New Testament Christians developed a rather elaborate system of eschatology which has kept biblical theologians busy to the dawning of the twenty-first century. A great deal has been written about the last and final judgment that will occur when God decides to end the world. According to the biblical record, the just shall be separated from the wicked (Matthew 13:47-50), the latter shall be punished (Matthew 13:29), and the entire world will be destroyed (II Peter 3:7-12). A new heaven and earth will be constructed after the old has been destroyed. According to one interpretation, God will then establish an earthly reign but only with those who have been faithful to His Gospel.

Native North Americans have frequently been the target of frivolous talk about eschatology with mention of the phrase "happy hunting ground." The phrase has been invented by non-Natives as a parallel to the Christian version of heaven, the abode of the deceased who lived justly (Eastman, 1980: 156). In fact, in traditional First Nations' theology there was no clear line of demarcation between human beings and the spirit world. It was quite possible for spirits to contact human beings and affect their daily activities. The human world was permeable by spirit-beings who entered the human domain and left at will. Some tribes also believed in reincarnation, that is, some people could die and return to the human world in another form.

Traditionally, Native North Americans believed in an active reciprocity between humans and the spirit world based on gifts and gratitude. Individuals would offer gifts to the spirits and in return would receive good crops or be successful on a hunt. Sometimes rituals would be attached to the act of gift-giving and their range would include everything from miraculous cures to various forms of daily blessings. Lowie (1952: 41) observed that the Crows believed after death souls descended underground to join the Earth Deity. Some spirits, however, could return to the world in exceptional cases. Due to the nature of their untimely or unusual death, some souls might linger on the earth for a period of time perhaps beseeching their survivors to be released. Some remained, however, and "haunted" specific locations. One Sioux

Reservation in North Dakota at Devil's Lake is believed to be one such location. The Sioux called the lake "Minnewaukan Seche" or "Spirit Waters," which was somehow translated as "Lake of the Evil Spirit" by incoming settlers.

The notion of contact with the spirits of the deceased is not restricted to the theology of Aboriginal Peoples, as mentioned in an earlier chapter. When Israel's first king, King Saul, fell into disfavor with the prophet, Samuel, who had just died, Saul became uneasy. He then consulted a spiritist, the Witch of Endor, to bring up the spirit of Samuel. Saul had to disguise himself for the occasion because as king he had banned the work of spiritists and mediums from his kingdom. The witch protested to his request, fearing it was trap, but after some coaxing on Saul's part she managed to bring up Samuel who "came up out of the ground" (I Samuel 28:13). As Samuel arose from his sleep he revealed great distress that Saul had sought him out. He conveyed the Lord God's message to Saul that the latter had been repudiated as king and his throne would be given to his successor, David. Not long after Saul took his own life by falling on his own sword (I Samuel 31:4).

The First Nations believed very much in an afterlife. As one elder told a Moravian missionary, "We Indians shall not forever die. Even the grains of corn we put under the earth grow up and become living things" (Spence, 1994: 127). Elaborate preparations were made for funerals particularly in the case of the aged when it was expected. The belief was so strong that individual graves were often stocked with items that the deceased might wish to make use of in the next world. The Sioux developed a sacred rite by which to purify the soul of the deceased to assure its final destination. One of their seven sacred rites, the rite of "The Keeping of the Soul" was given to the Sioux by the White Buffalo Cow Woman and implied that the soul could be kept in the proximate arena in which death occurred until it could be purified. In one enactment a lock of hair of a deceased child was taken and held in the fragrance produced by a glowing coal with sweetgrass on it. Prayers were said and when the ritual ended the lock was wrapped in sacred buckskin and placed in a special location in the teepee. The pipe was lighted and smoked and everyone present participated as the pipe was passed in a sunwise direction. After the pipe returned to the spiritual leader who initiated the rite, he cleansed the pipe in case an unworthy person had smoked it. Once the rite was completed the soul of the deceased could return immediately to the Great Spirit and no longer needed to wander aimlessly in the afterlife state (Brown, 1989: 10-13).

The notion of soul sleep was not unique to First Nations. When Jesus visited his friends, Mary and Martha, after their brother, Lazarus, had died (John 11: 1-44), Mary lamented that Jesus had arrived too late to help. She believed in Jesus' power to raise the dead, but she was sure that in this situation it was too late even for Him to perform a miracle. Jews believed that after death the soul hovers over the body for four days and then goes into the afterlife. By some miracle a person might be resurrected during the first three days but not after that. Mary believed that if Jesus had come earlier He might have been able to resurrect Lazarus, but now it was clearly too late. Biblical commentators believe that Jesus deliberately waited four days so that when He did resurrect Lazarus, everyone would know that it was truly a miracle of God's doing.

Ake Hultkrantz (1953: 37) was probably the first social scientist to make an extensive study of First Nations eschatology, but in keeping with his European sense of academic ethnocentrism, he labelled all Indian conceptions of the soul as "predominantly shallow and superficial". True, the exact dimensions and characteristics of the Indian hereafter were not carefully delineated, but since so little scientific evidence of exactness is available, their approach is probably the most scientifically-safe one to adopt. The future state of the soul was not a predominant issue with them; they perceived it as more important to live in keeping with the mandates of the Creator while they were on earth. It is also possible that the oral tradition influenced the rather vague conceptualizations that were passed on from generation to generation thereby being more adaptable to time and place (Friesen, 1977: 108). It is no secret that those who worship at the shrine of the written tradition have often been embarrassed when new light is shed on what has previously been regarded as scientifically solid truth.

# Nine

# Spiritual Leadership

Every cultural configuration studied by social scientists has been known to set aside a certain individual or group of people whose responsibility it has been to offer guidance on spiritual matters. This office has been called by various names – prophet, priest, minister, clergyman, elder, shaman, and so on. Individuals raised in a particular society with specific nomenclature regarding the office of spiritual leader or advisor often yield to the temptation of ethnocentrism when learning about that role in a cultural setting different from their own. The result is often to perceive differences that may emerge in less than complimentary ways. Christians, for example, are quite used to such terms as clergymen, preacher, priest or elder, but they cringe in ethnocentric fear when it is suggested that these roles could been seen as parallel to that of shamans in other cultural settings. It seems logical that if one can attach a different term to the same occurring phenomenon in a different cultural setting, one somehow becomes immune from having to consider its parallel function. In an effort to neutralize the subject so that a degree of objectivity may be attained, in this discussion the concept of elder will be preferred in reference to contemporary times because it appears to be less laden with negatively preconceived notions.

## The Concept Elaborated

The practice of recognizing and respecting special spiritual abilities on the part of leading men or women within a given cultural configuration is as old as human civilization. Knudtson and Suzuki (1992) note that the human tradition of designating certain individuals within a group as having leadership gifts in the spiritual domain goes back to the very origins of humankind. In contrast, the skepticism of the modern scientific mind that tends to doubt the efficacy of such status is of very recent origins. Unlike the traditional perspective, the scientific originated in the shallower soils of seventeenth century European Christianity and natural philosophy although some of its roots may go back as far as Judaistic and Greek thought.

A wide range of talents and abilities with regard to the role of spiritual leader may be outlined, some quite unique to a given cultural configuration, and others virtually universally recognized. Methods of recognizing spiritually-related offices also vary from culture to culture, and are identified via various processes, that is, heredity, apprenticeship or modelling, charisma or even by appointment or election. Differences that do occur in practice may often be explained by careful study. Each culture appears to have its own way of peoples ascribing such status and this is parallelled by the reality that individuals have unique ways of fulfilling such office.

One point of differentiation among these various offices that appears to have some merits is with regard to the recognition of individuals with spiritual abilities, gifts or insights versus individuals who may claim to possess magic-religious powers. According to anthropologists, the latter are usually called "shamans," and are most frequently identifiable in what have been called "primitive" societies (Eliade, 1974: 3). Unfortunately, as a result of this labelling, the term "shaman" is often taken to mean any magician, sorcerer, medicine man or women or ecstatic found throughout the history of religions and religious ethnology.

For example, an early anthropologist, Roland Dixon (1908: 7), described the medicine man as encompassing five distinct roles in "the lower stages of culture." Vogel (1990: 22) outlined a recognized breakdown among the Ojibway as comprising four ranks: (i) priests of the Midewiwin or medicine society; (ii) the Wabenos or "dawn men" who practised medicinal magic, hunting medicine and love powders; (iii) the Jessakid, who functioned as seers or prophets, and revealed hidden truths to the people; and, (iv) herbalists who generally dominated the field of the medicine man or woman. Undoubtedly, the functions of the latter group were primarily related to the arena of healing based a metaphysical or spiritual framework.

A complex breakdown of spiritual leadership among the Sioux is offered by Lame Deer and Erdoes (1972: 154f). Here five categories are defined: first is the *pejuta wicasa*, or man of herbs. This individual heals with herbs but he must also have the wakan (power of the Spirit) to do so. Second, the *waayatan* is a prophet, a man who can foretell future events. Third, the *wapiya* is a conjurer, often labelled witch doctor by anthropologists. This person can be either good or bad; he can either chase evil spirits that cause sickness out of the body or he can put sickness into a person and then charge to get rid of it. Fourth, the *heyoka,* who is a sacred clown, uses thunder power to cure people. Fifth, and finally, there is the only "true" medicine man known as the *wicasa wakan* who may be able to work cures, prophesy, talk to herbs, command stones and even change the weather. The *wicasa wakan* receives this power as the result of a vision. He loves silence and meditation and often prefers to be alone. This kind of medicine man is neither good nor evil; he is just himself. As Merkur (1990: 55) notes, quoting Rasmussen;

> The shaman does not get his power from the animal [spirit], but from a mysterious "power" in the air; at the same time as it is near to them it is so infinitely remote that it cannot be described. It is a power in the air, in the land, in the sea, far away and around them. Only the shaman knows about this power; he is the medium. He works on the mind and thoughts as much as he can.

The powers of the shamans are said to result not only from their experiences in the current life, but in Aboriginal cultures who believe in reincarnation, shamans could also receive endowments acquired during previous lives or between successive lives. The relationship between the dream, vision and spirit realm encountered within one life and experiences of the spirit realm encountered between lives, and over a succession of lives, is an area that continues to call for textual and linguistic analysis. Part of the difference in these realms emanates from the crucial difference between First Nations' eschatology and that which prevails in the western world. As with other aspects of Aboriginal spirituality, a clear understanding of the role of shaman has never been truly comprehended by western anthropologists. Hallowell (1942: 3), once noted;

> . . . even at best our comprehension of the belief system of a primitive people remains on the intellectual level. We never learn to feel and act as they do. Consequently, we never fully penetrate their . . . behavior world. We never wear their culturally-tinted spectacles; the best we can do is to try them on.

Hallowell reflected the insensitivity of his times when he referred to First Nations as "primitive," a clear indication of the patronizing tone of that era. It has taken some time for social scientists to develop more neutral descriptives for describing the Indigenous Peoples, that is, Aboriginal or First Nations. A similar tendency was prevalent with regard to Aboriginal spiritual beliefs which for a long time were described by western anthropologists and theologians as "myths." Tooker (1979: 31) observed that even though the observations of nature by Native peoples were no less acute and no less intellectual than those made by thinkers of the old world, they were relegated a lesser place simply by the assignment derogatory or offensive descriptives.

Among the Inuit (formerly called Eskimos) shamans have been identified as "someone who has the spirit," meaning that such an individual derives special powers from an extraordinary sphere. The shaman has access either by gift or training to an additional source of power besides psychological, mental, social or that derived from technique. The nature of the spirits could be good or evil, depending on their orientation. Evil spirits that had to be appeased by shamans were envisaged as residing in the form of human or animal ghosts who had been prevented from journeying to the afterlife, and shamans tried to hinder them from doing their malevolent or dangerous work. These "evil" spirits caused all manners of misfortune, accident, disease or death and required appeasement or control by capable shamans (Merkur, 1990: 49). A shaman with recognized power could inspire fear in the evil spirits and motivate them to leave their intended victims alone. Good spirits, on the other hand, could lend assistance to a hunter or a vision quester and thereby become worthy of thanks (Walker, 1991: 72).

Somewhat in contrast to the "magically oriented" role of shaman is the office of elder, a position usually ascribed to knowledgeable men or women, and so recognized for the gift of wisdom which they demonstrated – derived either as a gift, through apprenticeship, or through their own spiritual experiences. To add to the complexity of description it should be noted that these categories are not mutually exclusive. Those who are recognized as "spiritual" persons usually ascribe their powers to their relations with the spiritual world. Some may claim to be possessed by the spirits or even control them, particularly with regard to human behavior. To further complicate matters, there were charlatans or fakers who operated in connection with the healing arts, and sought to make a living by dishonest means. There were also some who imagined themselves to be human benefactors, doubtlessly deceived by some hapless good fortune in that respect. This phenomenon developed particularly at the time when Europeans began to arrive on this continent and many of the non-Natives newcomers began to make claims about having learned the tricks of "Indian medicine" and so peddled their "knowledge" among the early settlers. Vogel (1990: 137) describes one of the curing techniques for cancer used by an "Indian healer" named John Goodale Briante:

> Take "King of all Poison," pound up, pulverize it, bind it on the cancer, and it will take out all the inflammation. Then, use a wash made as follows: take hardwood ashes, bleach them and boil them down to the liquor till it is very strong. Apply this twice a day with a swab, to kill the cancer.

A unique individual spiritual gift sometimes recognized by members of a society is the ability to make prophesies, to foresee future cultural happenings or developments. Prophets usually engage in cautioning their colleagues about possible negative forthcoming events, and when their prognostications later prove to be accurate, their credentials are more firmly validated in the minds of societal members. Charles Eastman (1980: 157), a Sioux, observed that the oral tradition in his tribe documented the account that a prophet predicted the coming of the white man a full fifty years before the event occurred. Another prophet described the coming of the "Fire Boat" (steamboat), long before the vehicle actually appeared. Plains Indian history is rife with other examples affirming the gift of prophecy, often with regard to such matters as war, invasions or plagues. Before his death more than a century ago, Crazy Horse of the

Sioux prophesied that the dying teachings of the First Peoples would eventually be revived. The words of his prophetic song are:

> My friend, they will return again. All over the earth, they are returning again. Ancient teachings of the earth, ancient songs of the earth, they are returning again. My friend, they are returning. I give them to you, and through them you will understand, you will see. They are returning again upon the earth. (Kaltreider, 1998: 115)

## Spiritual Leadership in Aboriginal Culture

The tribal encampments of the traditional First Peoples were structured to meet the various needs of a large number of people. There were leading chiefs and subchiefs, councillors and hunting chiefs and a host of organized societies in place, all of which had specified duties and responsibilities. Since the underlying premise of Aboriginal society was spiritual, it is not surprising that there were also specified structures in place to accommodate religious needs. Commonly called sodalities, these formal organizations cut across kinship and band lines and featured administrative, policing and other duties. The type of sodality embracing the largest part of a band, tribe-let or state is properly called a tribal sodality. Most First Peoples in North America featured sodalities with the exception of the Arctic, Sub-Arctic, Plateau, Great Basin and Northeast Mexico. Among northwest coast tribes, more specifically oriented sodalities provided a mechanism for individuals to acquire supernatural power and at the same time acquire a high profile for themselves and maintain high position for their extended families in the tribal hierarchy (Driver, 1968: 410).

Often sodalities also played protective roles, for example, among the Kiowa the owner and keeper of the Sacred Arrows or the Sacred Hat belonged to a sacred organization. The Pottawatomi had a similar arrangement with regard to their Sacred Drum, and among many tribes were pipe holders who had affiliations to formal societies. Among more stable societies like the Arikara, Hidatsa and Mandans, social structures were more complex, tightly knit and comprehensive. Clan organizations played a central role, adding a degree of complexity to both the structure and functioning of their sodalities (Newcomb, 1974: 94f). The Arikara, Hidatsa and Mandan peoples operated a number of women's societies which had collective purchase features like those of the men, minus military or police duties. One such group was called the "Goose Women" whose responsibilities including the performance of ceremonies to ensure a good corn crop and attract buffalo to the camp. Another women's club was called "White Buffalo Cow Women," who also had a ritual to attract buffalo to their encampments.

In traditional Lakota culture, religious leaders worked together for the common spiritual good. No medicine man would place themselves above spiritual leaders in the same role or above others in the tribe. Lakota medicine men were humble, cooperative and caring. According to Pettipas (1994: 15),

Piapot, a Cree spiritual leader and healer, refused to take credit for the blessing of healing rains which he had helped bring about. He informed the gathering that his power to perform came from the strength of the people themselves and he advised that "only the whole community joining together can call on the Great Spirit to act in pity for us." As Curtis noted (Gifford, 1976: 29f), the Indian conception of healing was always

> through Divine power even though a healing agent could be instrumental is assisting the process. In the final analysis, the act of curing was usually accomplished amid song, ceremony, and prayer.

A biblically-recognized apostle and elder, St. Paul, made a plea to elders for humility in service when he wrote,

> Brethren, I do not consider myself yet to have taken hold of it. But one thing I do: Forgetting what is behind; and straining toward what is ahead, I press on toward the goal to win the prize for which God has called me heavenward in Christ Jesus. (Philippians 3:13)

He cautioned his peers in eldership with these words, "Whatever happens, conduct yourselves in a manner worthy of the gospel of Christ" (Philippians 1:27a). According to Powers (1990: 147), this was the traditional position of such elders as Black Elk whose role among his people, the Lakota, was greatly exaggerated by non-Native writers who made him out to be some sort of spiritual hero. Powers argues that Black Elk repudiated many of the things that were written about him, including the contents of the book, *Black Elk Speaks* (Neihardt, 1979) preferring to be remembered primarily as an Episcopalian catechist instead of some spiritual authority on traditional Sioux theology. If Powers is correct, then we shall have to look elsewhere for an explanation of the traditional role of Native elder.

Several reputable works about the specific role of elder in traditional Native societies include Beatrice Medicine's essay (1987), "My Elders Tell Me," Ruth Kirk's (1986) *Wisdom of the Elders*; Joseph Couture's (1991a) "The Role of Native Elders: Emergent Issues," and, Knudtson and Suzuki's (1992) *Wisdom of the Elders*. According to these sources, elders are making a comeback in Native societies, that is, their wisdom is again being sought out. Couture, a Cree elder, sees true elders as "superb embodiments of highly developed potential. They exemplify the kind of person which a traditional, culturally-based learning environment can and does form and mold" (Couture, 1991a: 207). Medicine (1987: 142), a Lakota elder, concurs, suggesting that "Elders are repositories of cultural and philosophical knowledge and are transmitters of such information". Traditionally, elders were always consulted in the tribal decision-making process and even political leaders relied on their advice in decision-making. Kirk (1986: 13) observes that Native elders have memories of the old days since they have lived the transition from past to present. This enables them to share meaningful insights about earlier Indian life.

Knudtson and Suzuki (1992) suggest that Native elders have a vital role to play in communicating a sense of the sacred to this generation. They argue that traditionally, the First Peoples lived as caretakers of all life. They believed that all living things that were created, and were given to the people, should be deemed precious. The role of the people was to protect and use all of these precious things wisely, and to share with them in order to keep harmony among all people. The concern of elders today is that society has gone too far in disrespecting nature and its rhythms. A return to the spiritual foundation of life is badly needed.

## Spiritual Leadership in the Old Testament

The advisory role of elder in the Old Testament was officially mandated by Moses on the suggestion of his father-in-law (Exodus 18:13-27). It seems that Moses regularly took a seat at the gate of the camp to listen to people's grievances and to offer them advice. This duty took him from morning till evening and he had little opportunity to fulfil his other obligations. His father-in-law, Jethro, noted this inefficiency on Moses' part and offered a suggestion.

> Why do you alone sit as judge, while all these people stand around you from morning till evening? ...What you are doing is not good. You and these people who come to you will only wear yourselves out. The work is too heavy for you; you cannot handle it alone. ... select capable men from all the people – men who fear God, trustworthy men who hate dishonest gain – and appoint them as officials over thousands, hundreds, fifties and tens. Have them serve as judges for the people at all times ... (Exodus 18: 14b,17b-18, 21-22a)

The roles of prophet and judge are not definitively separated in the Old Testament, and the individuals who fulfilled in these roles often served a multiplicity of functions. The role of elder was usually filled by older men who were heads of families and who had plenty of experience in the management of family affairs. Since written materials were scarce they were perceived as depositories of the traditions of bygone generations. Great reverence was awarded the elderly among the Hebrews and old age was regarded as synonymous with wisdom, knowledge and experience and as a reward for having lived a virtuous and godly life (Deuteronomy 32:7, Job 12:12, Proverbs 16:31). This was the command of God, to wit, "Rise in the presence of the aged, show respect for the elderly and revere your God. I am the Lord" (Leviticus 19:32).

Prior to the time that Israel aspired to official nationhood and was thereafter served by kings, a succession of judges emerged to serve the people with the Lord's approval (Judges 2:16). Because of the complexity of their roles, these individuals were also called prophets. The first mentioned judge was Othneil who was Caleb's younger brother. Caleb, along with Joshua, had served as one of twelve spies who checked out Jericho, but only he and Joshua had faith that Israel could claim the promised land (Numbers 13:30). Othneil was succeeded by Ehud (Judges 3:15), Shamgar (Judges 3:31), and Deborah, the first female judge (Judges 4:4), who was also known as a prophetess. She held court under a palm tree and prophesied that the army of Israel under the leadership of Barak would crush the army of Canaan. After a successful battle the land was in peace for forty years. Deborah was followed by Gideon, who took an army of three hundred trumpeters against thousands of Midianites and defeated them with a surprise attack (Judges 7:22-25). Easily the most publicized career of an Israelite judge by Hollywood was that of Samson, but movies do not often tell the real story. His story is told in the Book of Judges in three chapters (Judges 13-16).

Perhaps the best-known and best-loved Hebrew elder was Samuel who received his call to ministry as a child. According to the biblical record Samuel's mother, Hannah, had difficulty conceiving, and she promised that if Jehovah would give her a son she would immediately return him to the temple where he would serve as an altar boy (I Samuel 1:22). In all his affairs, Samuel remained true to the Lord and sought His advice in all things. He was a patriotic man but did not seek power for himself, and when the people cast him aside "because of his grey hairs" he did not complain. Later Samuel had the dubious distinction of anointing the first (Saul) and second (David) kings of Israel though he was not exactly excited about the idea of giving the Hebrews a king. Israel, however, wanted a king so they could be like other nations (I Samuel 8:5) and with Jehovah's approval, Samuel eventually gave in. In his final speech Samuel warned the Hebrews to obey the Lord at all times, and as an added incentive to back his warnings, he called on the Lord to send thunder and rain upon the people (I Samuel 12:18). Oddly, most Christians readily accept this ability of Samuel's part as perfectly within reason but have difficulty in believing that an Aboriginal spiritual leader could do the same.

The prophetic office did not disappear in Israel with the anointing of kings. Nathan, for example, appears on the scene when he advises King David to built a temple unto the Lord (II Samuel 7:2-3). One day David noticed that he lived in a palace of cedar while the holy Ark of the Covenant remained in a tent. Jehovah then told Nathan to inform David that it was quite proper for him to build a temple to store the ark. David subsequently had a vision from the Lord telling him that it would be inappropriate for him, a man of war, to build the temple. That would be done by his son and successor, King Solomon.

Nathan's second appearance in the Bible occurs when he undertakes the distasteful task of informing the favored monarch that he had committed a heinous sin (II Samuel 12:1-14). David, it seems, had fallen in love with Bathsheba, a married woman, whom he had seen bathing outside his palace window. He arranged for her husband, Uriah, to be sent to the enemy front lines and lo and behold, he was conveniently killed. David then added Bathsheba to his harem. Even then powerful men were not safe from the

Lord's hand of justice and Nathan was selected to accost the king about his actions. Nathan did so, and probably to his surprise, David assumed responsibility for his crime and broke down to confess. Nathan told David a parable (legend) to get the king's attention. It was about a poor man who only owned a little ewe lamb. A rich man, who had many flocks, however, took the little lamb from the poor man so that he had nothing at all. On hearing the story David immediately threatened to punish the wicked man if he was within his kingdom; then suddenly realized that the target of the story was himself. In answer to David's query as to the whereabouts of the guilty man, Nathan said, "You are the man!" (II Samuel 12:7a). The text of the thirty-second psalm reveals the nature of David's tremendous guilt and subsequent repentance:

> For day and night your hand was heavy upon me; my strength was sapped
> as in the heat of summer. Then I acknowledged my sin to you and did not
> cover up my iniquity. I said, "I will confess my transgressions to the Lord"
> – and you forgave the guilt of my sin. (Psalm 32: 4-5)

Couture (1991a: 202) insists that as the Aboriginal spiritual renaissance gets underway, Native elders are again being listened to – this time by both Natives and non-Natives. If this is so, there may yet be time to initiate some of the reforms recommended by this rare group of individuals, namely to find an earth response to an earth problem. "We need only to listen to what Mother Earth is telling us" about pollution, contamination, consumption, misuse and draining of resources, and so on (Couture, 1991a: 209).

## Spiritual Leadership in the New Testament

Theologians tend to ground New Testament doctrines in both Old Testament history and practice. Thus the beliefs, rituals and practices of Old Testament Israel have a direct bearing on New Testament church structure and liturgy. The role of elder is evident in both the Gospels and the writings of St. Paul even though the selection of such office is amended with the establishment of congregations by Paul and his missionary colleagues. When Jesus' parents, Mary and Joseph, brought Jesus to the temple for circumcision they were greeted by the prophet Simeon who was a "righteous and devout" man (Luke 2:25). Simeon had been waiting for word that the Messiah had come and it had been revealed to him that he would not die until he had seen this hope become a reality. Later the family met a prophetess named Anna who lived permanently in the temple worshipping day and night, praying and fasting (Luke 2:36-37). She too recognized Jesus as the promised one and readily gave her blessing to the event.

After the crucifixion and death of Jesus Christ his disciples set about establishing Christianity as an organized religion. Although he was not one of the original twelve disciples, St. Paul (originally called Saul), joined the movement and quickly brought structure and order to the rapidly growing phenomenon. He and his colleagues, Barnabus, Silas and John Mark, went about establishing churches in areas surrounding Israel and appointed elders to serve in local congregations and "with prayer and fasting, committed them to the Lord, in whom they had put their trust" (Acts 14:23). In doing this they followed the pattern of Jesus who, after he had selected twelve disciples to serve as legal witnesses to his cause, also appointed others to spread the good news of the Gospel. The Gospel of Luke records that "After this the Lord appointed seventy-two others and sent them two by two ahead of him to every town and place where he was about to go" (Luke 10:1).

The office of apostle may be differentiated in scripture from that of elder in that the former appears to have had more organizational responsibility and status. Apostles were more likely people who were sent on special missions in the sense that Paul and Barnabus were sent out by the head church at Antioch to establish additional congregations. They were given authority to appoint elders who were spiritual leaders selected to serve local churches. Elders had to be spirit-filled individuals who could relieve the Apostles for their preaching duties by being responsible for such tasks as counselling, waiting on tables (at feasts), distributing food and looking after the needs of widows and orphans (Acts 6:2-4).

The parallel function of elder in Native society to that of Old Testament practice is quite evident. In Aboriginal circles today the phrase "My elders tell me" is almost a watchword. Elders are being consulted much in the spirit with which the people of Israel sought out Moses' guidance at the gate (Exodus 18:13-14). This is done on an individual basis as well as in a more formal fashion. For example, for the past thirty years Native elders from all over North America have met at the Stoney Campground at Morley, Alberta, for the Annual Indian Ecumenical Conference. The campground is located approximately fifty kilometres west of Calgary on the Stoney (Nakoda Sioux) Indian Reserve (Snow, 1977:142). At its peak in the 1970s, the conference drew more than seven thousand people, but its numbers have decreased since financial resources are less plentiful today. For ten days each year elders still continue to consult, pray and share ideas with each other and with members of the younger generation who attend.

The New Testament model of elder functioning is also in vogue among First Nations today. Examples of this reality abound. Recently a pipe-carrier of Blackfoot ancestry told me that she is constantly reminded by elders that she must avoid adopting non-Native ways and walk worthy of her Aboriginal calling. A Stoney friend mentioned that his tribe would never think of conducting any public ceremony without the prayers of at least one elder. When the sundance was recently reintroduced to the Siksika People the instigators for reinstatement first sought the approval of elders before proceeding. The All Native Circle Conference of the United Church of Canada only meets with the approval and presence of recognized elders from the various tribes who are represented within the conference. The Native Centre of the University of Calgary regularly arranges for spiritual ceremonies to be conducted by recognized elders who also make themselves available for consultation with students. Young people pursuing careers often meet with elders on a one-to-one basis to seek out spiritual direction for their lives. Finally, as Medicine (1987) points out, since First Nations do not segregate spirituality from politics, some Native political leaders are seeking out elders on major matters before they make decisions about them. A number of schools also employ the services of elders for language and cultural teaching, spiritual guidance and consultation.

While society today appears to be on a quest for sexual and age equity in every way, the wisdom of the elders is increasingly being sought out by the First Nations. In their quest they appear to be coming more closely in line with the biblical model. Elder stories and sayings also bear a resemblance to scriptural injunctions. This observation may be illustrated by the following sayings:

> There are only two things you have to remember about being Indian. One is that everything is alive, and the second is that we are all related. . . . It's up to you; you have all the answers within you. What is life but a journey into the Light. At the center of Life is the Light. . . . Soon I will cross the River, go up the Mountain, into the Light. (Couture, 1991a: 61, 205)

Thus, the search continues.

# Ten

# Comments on Stoney (Nakoda Sioux) Metaphysics: A Case Study

This chapter is an impressionistic version of Stoney beliefs and practices as I have witnessed them over a period of more than three decades as a visitor and researcher in the community. This includes fourteen years as minister of the local congregation, the Morley United Church. These experiences form the basis of my accumulated insights concerning the spiritual orientation of this unique community.

Historians are generally agreed that the Stoney Tribe separated from the Yanktonai branch of the Sioux and became known as Assiniboines. They travelled north sometime between 1640 and 1658 during which time they were mentioned as a separate tribe in diaries penned by Jesuit priests (Dempsey, 1988: 43). Another interpretation intimates that they migrated west along with the fur trade as a means of escaping the impact of the dreaded diseases that accompanied European settlement (Friesen, 1995a, 74). According to one of several different versions of their own oral tradition, however, the Stoneys have always lived in the area they now occupy. Stoney Chief John Snow (1977: 20) states, "They did not consider that we had lived here for thousands of years, even ten thousands of years, without money and without a written law."

The Stoney tribal population approaches 3 500 people who live in three bands (Bearspaw, Chiniki and Wesley), and are located on three reservations (in Canada the word "reserve" is used) in south-central Alberta. The name of the tribe probably originated with explorers because of the unique Assiniboine method of preparing broth. After digging a hole in the ground, they lined it with a clean piece of rawhide, then added water which they heated with hot stones from a nearby fire. When the desired temperature was reached, the meat was added. Stoney Indians were literally "cookers with stones."

The Stoney people are an atypical tribe in that they, more than any other Alberta plains tribe, still live very much in accordance with their traditional philosophy and lifestyle. As a people who have labored hard to preserve and perpetuate their ancient ways the Stoneys have succeeded where others have failed. This is particularly noteworthy because of their close proximity to a large urban center from which influences they remain relatively unaffected.

One of the first European records pertaining to the Stoneys came from the pen of explorer Alexander Henry the Younger who noted in his journal that the Stoneys were great buffalo hunters and very hospitable to strangers. Unlike other Plains Indian tribes who chased the buffalo on horseback or used buffalo jumps as a means of killing the animals, the Stoneys built impoundments for trapping the bison, then chased the lumbering beasts into them and shot them at will.

## Missionary Activity

A Methodist missionary, Robert T. Rundle, arrived in the Morley vicinity around 1840 and immediately attracted Stoney followers. The traditional Stoney approach was to receive outsiders graciously, listen to their ideas and then incorporate elements of what they deemed to be useful concepts into the thought-patterns of their own philosophy. As the historical record shows, undoubtedly the Stoneys underestimated the nature and future impact of the Methodist message. It represented more than a congenial sharing of spiritual ideas; the inherent missionary mandate was to take over and redesign Stoney values to fit a European anglo-Christian mould. Despite the missionaries' best efforts, however, this objective has never been realized even to this day.

In 1873, other Methodist missionaries, the Reverend George McDougall and his son, John, built a permanent mission among the Stoneys along the Bow River at Morley (Sibbald, 1971: 1). The building of the mission tended to polarize the three Stoney bands in the region, and the McDougalls eventually supervised the building of a church, a schoolhouse and an orphanage in the settlement (Ironside and Tomasky, 1971: 20). The original church building still stands on the reserve as a memorial to McDougall's efforts although a newer edifice, erected in 1921, serves the community under the auspices of the United Church of Canada.

Despite their reverence for their traditional ways, the Stoneys are keenly interested in associating with, sharing and learning from other Indigenous tribes. When the first Annual Indian Ecumenical Conference was held at the Crow Agency in Montana in 1970, the Stoney chiefs and council invited the conference to Morley for the next annual event. Since then the conference has been held annually at the Stoney Indian Park on the Stoney Reserve.

When his father, George, died in a prairie blizzard, John McDougall carried on with missionary work among the Stoneys. He premised his mandate on the slogan, "Christianize, educate and civilize" (Friesen, 1974a). In his efforts to Christianize the Indians, he tried to convince them that the Christian Gospel provided sources of inspiration and power which were responsible for the white man's success and eminence. His rather uncomplicated assumption that adherence to Christianity would produce economic prosperity correlated with his attempts to convince the Indians that any efforts to oppose the government's plans to populate Indian lands with European settlers were wrong and must be opposed.

A fundamental aspect of McDougall's mission was his allegiance to the British Crown, a concept entwined with the idea of loyalty and obedience to God and country (Friesen, 1974b). His sermons reflected an admixture of Christian doctrine mingled with an admonition to respect and obey governmental or municipal orders, and adopt a European form of civilization. It was his conviction that the latter was somehow derived from an orderly obedience to Christian precepts coupled with the conviction that the British system was an outstanding example of political and economic success. He described the reaction to this mission as follows:

> Sometimes the Chief would ask me to tell about white men and how they conducted matters. I would respond with a short address on government and municipal organization, or at another time speak of civilization and some of its wonders, or give a talk on education. . . . (McDougall, 1898: 75)

McDougall's objective in "civilizing" the Stoneys was to be achieved primarily through literacy. The attainment of this skill would enable the Indians to learn to read and thus attain biblical knowledge for themselves. He hoped that this process would eventually influence them into adopting his notion of an orderly, democratic system of governing local affairs. McDougall either had little knowledge of or no appreciation for the Stoneys' traditional method of arriving at decisions which was by talking them through to consensus. He probably assumed that their approach to problem solving was inefficient and could certainly be improved upon. McDougall did admit, however, that elements of his own heritage were faulty. He stated that it was hard to understand how some Europeans, themselves products of a "superior" civilization, could deliberately set out to destroy Indian culture by so unabashedly peddling liquor. Clearly these whiskey peddlers had forgotten their origins and training and were now being motivated purely by lust and greed. McDougall simply could not bring himself to agree with this stance. As he phrased it:

> How often it is borne in upon me that our civilization as it is called does not produce the gentleman, and even the higher influence of Christianity must struggle with our race to make real men and women. (McDougall, 1911: 33)

It was to McDougall's credit that he publicly denounced the liquor trade which made significant inroads among the Stoney people, even though he was usually quite defensive about the balance of his heritage and culture. His courage and credibility in agitating for the abolition of liquor is acknowledged by Stoney leaders to this day (Snow, 1977: 21). McDougall consistently employed a vocabulary of equity; he claimed that all persons were created equal, and insisted that mutual respect was to be the ground for effective human relations (Friesen, 1974a). He denounced the practice of Indian name-calling by employees at the fur-trading posts; Indian men were not "bucks," he insisted, and Indian women were not "squaws." (McDougall, 1911: 257). In addition, he advocated that Native and non-Native individuals should be able to relate to one another, not because of their differing race or station, but because of the benefits to be derived from learning about each others' cultural outlooks.

There is some difficulty in attempting to reconcile John McDougall's claims of adhering to a liberal human philosophy with his actions when living among the Stoneys. He was always very insistent that the Stoneys learn the white man's ways of civilization, and roundly denounced specific Stoney practices. He was disgusted at the performance of the "wolf feast," which consisted of a gathering of about two dozen men seated in a buffalo lodge, each having before him a large wooden dish of thick soup made of boiled slices of buffalo meat and wild lily roots. He described it as follows:

> When each man was served, an old medicine man began to chant in an unknown tongue, accompanying himself by swinging his rattle. By and by, all who were to partake joined his song of blessing. This over, each one drew his big bowl to him and at the signal put both hands into it for chunks of meat, pulled these to pieces and then began to cram the contents of the dish down his throat. While doing this, each one made a noise like the growling of a wolf. (McDougall, 1898: 91)

The event clearly nauseated McDougall and he labelled it a "beastly orgy," without affording its purpose much investigation. Evidently, the criterion for its denunciation was the fact that McDougall himself did not understand or simply could not be bothered to investigate its origins or significance. Despite his allegedly egalitarian perspective he was unable to operationalize his stated philosophy beyond the level of verbal proclamation.

## Stoney World View

In common with other Plains Indian tribes, Stoney Indians share a sense of a common, largely taken-for-granted everyday world. Its governance is in the hands of a supernatural Being – the Great Spirit, Wakâ Tâga, Creator or Sky father – who designed, created and manages the world for his children (Harrod, 1992: 24). John Snow, Chief of the Wesley Band of the Stoney Nation, speaks of the Great Spirit in the masculine singular;

> Our society was built around the concept of that the Great Spirit is the Supreme Being, the Great Mystery; recognizing Him as the One who provides all things was the first step and beginning of our tribal society." (Snow, 1977: 5)

Traditionally, the Creator was envisaged as occupying a high realm in the sky, and between Him and the earth He created was the domain of the spirits, eagles, thunder and lightning, and the heavenly bodies. It was to the spirits of this middle realm that warriors traditionally prayed and from whom they contrived means by which to discover their own spiritual identity. The spirits influenced the daily challenges of hunting and gathering, intra-tribal relations and inter-tribal interactions, but the underlying forces for their operation were set in motion by the Creator. Daily bargaining with the spirits sometimes resulted in visions, auditions and vivid dreams. The spirits were frequently considered to possess somewhat variableness of character, thus causing rivers to dry up, inspiring warriors, defeating the enemy, or turning the path of wandering buffalo (Burland, 1965). The spirit of an animal was entreated and thanked before the creature was taken for food. The plant spirit was contacted when a plant was utilized for medicinal or spiritual purposes. Spiritual forces caused the sun to rise and set, the grass to grow in the field and the storms to gather in the sky (Friesen, 1977: 104f).

Like their Sioux counterparts further south, the Stoneys held strongly to the notion of the interconnectedness of all life, a belief expanded to the conviction that these relationships extend further and further out from the individual to the immediate family, the extended family, the band, the clan and the tribal group. These relationships do not stop with the human realm but are connected to every life form in the universe including the environment, the land, animals, plants and the elements – sky, wind, fire, clouds and heavenly bodies (Brown, 1997: xiii). Envisaging no dichotomy between sacred and secular, the tribe still perceives and expects potential messages from the Creator in every being and object, animate and inanimate.

The Stoney reverence for the workings of nature as a potential teaching environment is still in place. Animals frequently roam free on the reserve and occasionally herds of horses, cattle and even swine invade the area of the townsite. Elders who offer public prayers will freely mingle various elements in their expressed thoughts including references to the Great Spirit, His gifts of living wildlife, and traditional ceremonies. Usually these prayers are concluded "in Jesus name," a fitting Christian ending. This approach is indicative of a much deeper appreciation of the links between the Creator and His various forms of creation with Stoney traditions. Trying to comprehend the implications of this perspective influences one to ponder what might have happened if the first European invaders had been open to investigating this form of Weltanschauung instead of being so anxious to remake it.

It was mentioned earlier that the reason the Stoneys accepted the white man's religion so quickly, and as a result made several significant shifts in their ways of governance, was because its basic premises were so akin to their own beliefs (Snow, 1977: 17). The Stoney's lived according to a high code of morality, and practised brotherhood, honesty and sharing, all in a form quite parallel to that postulated by orthodox Christian believers. Even though proponents of EuroAmerican-inspired forms of government did not recognize its composition and functioning, the Stoneys were a people with a distinct civilization and a long, structurally enriched heritage. They lived according to their own moral laws, and comprised a caring society. They were not greatly stratified and no one went hungry. They were a deeply spiritual people and celebrated a great many religious rituals. When their children began to talk and understand things, one of the first lessons they learned had to do with respecting the Great Spirit and fulfilling their responsibilities within the created world.

Essentially the tone of Stoney spirituality was positive, intrinsic, comprehensive and much akin to Christianity. Until the missionaries arrived the Stoneys did not have a word for "sin" nor a word for "hell." Equivalents for these words had to be invented (Snow, 1977: 7). The tribe strongly believed in prayer, the afterlife and the responsibility of the devout to manifest bravery, kindness, sharing and survival in their daily lives. They also believed very much in the benefits of natural medicine premised on the notion that if something in the environment could harm people, the Great Spirit would also provide a special herb to cure the sickness, or bless some other person with the wisdom to heal it.

## Stoney Spirituality

The parallels of Stoney theological beliefs with those of the imported European religious system appear to have been ignored by the missionaries. In fact, it seems they did not even bother to investigate whether there were any. The established form of culturally inculcating the young via modelling, informal apprenticeship or instruction by elders was ignored, and quickly replaced by a systematized form of rhetoric as well as the forced memorization of esteemed Methodist codes. Educators took no cognizance of Stoney ways, and although the Stoneys admiringly interwove elements of the new order into their own world view, essentially their traditional ways persisted. To outsiders, many of the internal meanings of Stoney rituals remain a mystery for Stoney leaders have often been reluctant to elaborate on their traditional values for fear they may be misunderstood. There is also in place an unspoken rule that only those who are qualified to do so have that privilege, and these individuals believe that an elucidation of revered beliefs can take place only at appropriate times, in specified locations and only through approved channels such as the telling of legends. It is never done in European-delineated systematic terms nor by unauthorized individuals. No one seizes power nor steps out of place in talking about spiritual beliefs; that right has historically been granted exclusively to recognized elders by the tribe through an informal process of authorization, usually over a long period of time. It has long been believed that explaining the Stoney belief system to outsiders is a risky business because it may so easily be misunderstood or appreciated by those not familiar with their traditional reasoning process.

When it becomes possible under certain circumstances to access information about aspects of traditional Stoney values through the courtesy of recognized spokespersons, one quickly gets the impression of a strong reverence for the past. Stoney Elders speak respectfully of their past society where spirituality was paramount. As a very traditional people, the old Stoney way was to view the universe as peopled with spirits approved by the Great Spirit who could offer aid to its occupants. Since they have also regarded themselves as "Christians" for the past century, the tribe has adopted Christian stories into their own mythology. Early in this century, they were described by missionaries as a Christian and peaceful tribe, and even today the United Church of Canada is the most commonly recognized form of organized religion on the Stoney Reserve at Morley, Alberta.

Stoney metaphysics is often misunderstood by outsiders and from time to time has been labelled as being based on superstitions by individuals who have shown little appreciation for spiritual channels other than their own. The spirits of the universe, existent in all animate and inanimate forms, were traditionally regarded as malleable by the Stoneys; they could provide or take away food and cause illness, good fortune or bad fortune. As Rodnick (1938) described it, nothing was unknown to these spirits and no event was beyond their power to control or change. They comprised the unseen hands that fashioned things, that made existence possible for all things.

Garner (1966) has suggested that the Stoney orientation to the spirit world traditionally manifested itself in various forms of "magic" (some researchers call it "psychological perception"), including "love magic." The process of magic is defined in terms of human interaction in which individuals believe that they may directly offset nature and each other, for good or ill, by their own efforts as distinct from appealing to Divine powers by sacrifice or prayer. The precise mechanism may not be understood by the participants but this does not hinder their resolve (Middleton, 1967). Magic was sometimes used as a manipulative device. Charges were once made against a Stoney woman by members of the Peigan tribe in the case of a cross-cultural marriage between a Peigan and Stoney arguing that she had employed magic as a means of having influencing her prospective Peigan spouse to get married (Garner, 1966). This practice is also utilized in relation to everyday events where the mover wishes to influence another individual to act in a certain manner or engage in a specific form of behavior.

Long (1961) suggests that an established Assiniboine courtship practice was for young men to pay fees to medicine men or women to charm desired maidens so they would return the suitor's affection. The love medicine was administered either with or without ceremony, and there were many charms available for such purpose. These may have been formed of a mixture of herbs and objects which were placed in a small ornamental bag, and carried on the person during courtship. If the rules were not followed with precision the charm would not work.

Perhaps the best contemporary concept by which to describe this category of activity is the notion of "using the powers of medicine" by which either good medicine or bad medicine may be practised as a means of influencing others. The intensity of the strength of the medicine power (still sometimes called "evil eye"), varies with the individual who, with successful practise, is said to have "strong medicine." The nature of good or evil is determined in the context of the tribe, "good," being defined as in its best interests, and "evil," being viewed as constituting contrary purposes. Naturally, there are also spiritual implications in its use. These subjects are not usually held up in discussion because they represent the taboo world of the spirits. Even talking about this matter puts the individual in jeopardy for having dared to tread in the realm of the forbidden. Undoubtedly, because of the alien manner in which the practice of evil eye is viewed by the outside world, and the Stoney reluctance to discuss its operations, there can be little hope that a better understanding of the phenomenon will result.

Plains First Nations other than the Stoneys also believe very strongly in the existence of "good" and "bad" medicine. Men and women who practise good medicine and who can teach the old ways are much in demand in Indian communities across the country. According to Ross (1992), those who practice bad medicine among the Ojibway and remain in their local communities inspire dread and fear. At times ceremonies are enacted to rid an individual of negative influence. The spiritual dimension continues to play a major part in the ongoings of many different tribes across Canada, and despite the fact that their connective rituals were banned for a long time, in some tribes they are making a strong comeback.

Belief in evil spirits is not restricted to Aboriginal history. In the New Testament Jesus was known to cast out evil spirits on occasion. In one instance he exorcised an evil spirit called "Legion" (meaning, "we are many"), out of a man and sent the demons into a herd of pigs who promptly rushed over a steep bank into a lake and drowned (Mark 5:11-13). On another occasion, Jesus healed a demon-possessed man who was blind and mute (Matthew 12:22). The people were astonished, but the moral legalists of the day, the Pharisees, did not like this action and labelled the action Jesus took as an evil thing. "But when the Pharisees heard this, they said, 'It is only by Beelzebub, the prince of demons, that this fellow drives out demons'" (Matthew 12:24). It is a certainty that an ample collection of such skeptics could also be identified today.

## Contemporary Practices

An informal label to Stoney perceptions of time, and sometimes joked about by tribal members themselves, is "Stoney time," a concept implying that the movement of clocks is not greatly revered on the reserve. Stoneys view the universe as circular, and all events such as the seasons are somehow connected to this paradigm. Seasons, in reality, do not necessarily begin each year on the same day nor even in the same week or month. In Western Canada, it sometimes appears that the weather rarely follows any particular pattern and, being naturalists, the Stoneys have simply applied this principle to the realm of human behavior. An event begins when "everyone is ready to start" – which means little to the non-Native outsider. Winter may be said to be in session when the temperature drops, water freezes and quite a bit of snow falls to the ground. A similar pattern is followed by the closing of a season or, for that matter, the end of a meeting. Everyone goes home "when it is time." Spring may be said to appear when the snow melts, the birds chirp and the crocus blooms. A meeting begins when "enough" people are gathered, and concludes when pretty well everyone has gone home.

Of course there are also corollary technicalities to observe in connection with the protocol of public occasions. A pow-wow will begin with the ceremonial march (grand entry) by the chiefs and Elders, but not necessarily at the announced time. Weddings almost always start later than the announced time, but since the guests understand that "this is how it is," no one is surprised or frustrated by a two hour wait at a wedding except, perhaps, the uninformed non-Native guests who may be in attendance. Some weddings may be totally or partially subsidized by the respective chief and band; thus it is possible that a wedding reception may have more people in attendance than were at the wedding ceremony. Wedding ceremonies may be attended by invitation, but an occasion to celebrate, like a wedding reception where there is food to eat, that is a community event. The community regards occasions featuring dining as automatically open to all. Good times are to be enjoyed and shared. Chances are that the band chief and council contributed toward the expense, which is especially apparent if the reception is being held in a more "public place." Good chiefs provide for their people.

Funerals in Stoney country highlight the tribe's disposition to respect the circle of life. Death is as vital and inevitable a link in the human chain of existence as birth, but it is that – a link, not a terminal point. This does not mean that the dead are not mourned, for indeed they are. Death, however has a different quality about it. It is not viewed with quite the same degree of finality or regret that characterizes many non-Indian funerals. It is an expected event for everyone. The procedure for funerals is not radically different from that practiced in most rural areas across Canada except that preceding the funeral itself the body of the deceased will lie in state in the family home for two or three days and relatives and friends will come to pay their respects at the wake. Services will be conducted in the home both before and after the body is brought to the home from the funeral home. The casket is usually opened for viewing in the home and anyone who would like to pay their last respects can do so by touching or shaking the hand of the deceased and perhaps offering a prayer (Ear, n.d.).

On the third or fourth day after the wake, a public funeral service will be held in the local church. At the end of a Stoney funeral church service, which lasts at least two or three hours, it usually takes a long time to say goodbye to the departed. After all, time is irrelevant when it comes to worthy events. The casket is again opened for viewing, and everyone in attendance forms a line and takes time to file by, extend condolences to the family, and bid farewell to the dead. Many touch the body, whispering words of goodbye; a few may kiss the deceased, and all linger. No one is in a rush to speed the line through except on an occasion where a loved one may be so overcome with grief that it becomes necessary for someone to put an arm around the individual and urge them away from the casket. When a service has two hundred to three hundred people in attendance, the procession to pay last respects may take an additional hour or two. There is always a great deal of hand-shaking with family members at Stoney funerals and the act is interpreted as a token of friendship and engaged in as a special form of commemoration for the one who has passed on.

At the burial site the scene is similarly unhurried. Many people stay at the graveside for an hour or more after the service even after the grave has been filled in. Volunteers fill the dirt back into the dug grave with shovels, usually young men who may wish to impress future in-laws by their eagerness. Conversely, young women will volunteer for cooking and cleaning duties as a means of gaining favor with their prospective in-laws (Ear, n.d.). A year later a feast will be sponsored in honor of the deceased.

The explicitly stated basis for the extended stay at the graveside is respect for the dead, but there is also the implicit rationale that worthy events simply deserve a "sufficient amount of time." The dictum seems to be, "When it is appropriate to do so, take all the time that is required." In such a context, time per se is irrelevant. When set in the context of the totality of human existence, however, in Stoney reasoning, the question is germane: "what is to be gained by cutting short a meaningful event and scurrying back to the treadmill of modern day routine?"

It is probably safe to conjecture that the majority of Stoneys today combine elements of Christianity into their personal traditional belief system. Pow-wows, pipe ceremonies, tobacco offerings and sweetgrass ceremonies are frequently celebrated although Christian terminology is evident in the language employed in these ceremonies. Most families choose to have their children baptized in the local United Church and most weddings are held there as well. Traditional singing and drumming are frequently part of a wedding ceremony or a funeral. Traditional elders serve a vital role in church services and are often invited to speak at different occasions or offer a blessing or a prayer for the sick.

A number of Christian groups other than the United Church of Canada function on the reservation, only one of which has a permanent building in the area. Generally speaking, these groups tend to condemn traditional Native spirituality and are committed to winning converts away from what they perceive to be a negative influence. At best this perspective has confused individuals who have been taught to believe that the old ways could not have been so bad since the Creator appears to have blessed the nation for so many centuries.

## Cultural Transformation

As the beginning of the twenty-first century develops, a number of looming factors, mainly economic, are prophetic in predicting immense changes for the Stoney Nation. Undoubtedly these will impact heavily on various aspects of Stoney society in the form of government-supported financial cutbacks and other infringements on Stoney economic operations. Social programs will likely also be targeted. In the meantime, the onslaught of social and technological forces, inherent in dominant society, will simultaneously continue to encourage further change. To illustrate this a series of contrasts between several fundamental societal values and the prevailing (and changing) Stoney orientation must be considered. It is helpful to note that throughout the campaign by colonial educators and missionaries to amend Stoney society there was little success. It is likely that the campaign will continue albeit the faces of the campaigners have changed to a less religious motif. In the meantime the Stoney Indians will undoubtedly continue to struggle on a number of fronts to ward off what they see as undesirable elements of white man's culture. Most aspects of the traditional way will likely prevail, others will be modified and those already severely affected by modern trends will possibly vanish completely – perhaps even be erased from the "annals" of the oral tradition.

The Stoney penchant to resist hard work for its own sake will likely prevail, premised on the notion that messing with the universe for no apparent good reason is not spiritually edifying. North Americans generally value a "doing society," and its operational changes are often brought about by social or technological forces induced by individual or group action. Whether the action is justified or not appears to make little difference. It is strongly believed that problems resulting from any kind of societal transformation can systematically be resolved by identifying the cause, studying the means of solution, deciding on a plan of action and then implementing it. "Getting

things done" is virtue to a non-Native because "doing" is always more important than "being" or "becoming."

The Stoney response to this concept is that "there had better be a good reason" backing demands for action. In addition, any proposed change should be
leader-initiated, tradition-consistent, community (tribally) approved and "we
had better like it." Reinforced by strong sanctions and taboos, the Stoney pre-
disposition to reject action for its own sake will likely also characterize the
Stoney culture of the twenty-first century.

According to the traditional post-Industrial Revolutionary perspective of
western civilization, the primary function of the universe is for its component
parts to be exploited and controlled by huhumankind in the interests of attain-
ing "the good life." This process inherently continues because it is believed
that the quality of the good life will  perpetually improve as a result. Humans
are masters of the universe, and nature can be conquered to accommodate
human needs. To actively attack problems of geography, topography and cli-
mate, in the interests of "the good life," are both commendable and justifiable
pursuits.

While traditional Stoney philosophy cautions humanity not to meddle
with natural processes, there is ample evidence that some modern forms of
technology which damage the universe through pollution (like trucks and
cars), are much valued by individual members of the tribe. Nearly all Stoney
people drive automobiles, and most of them make frequent shopping trips to
the nearby city of Calgary. In addition, the representative trash piles of modern society, indicative of the workings of a throw-away society are ample in
Stoney country. Plastic wrappings, cigarette boxes and empty pop bottles dot
the countryside, offering evidence of a consumer society, but coupled with the
traditional concept that nature will provide a way of taking care of the trash.
This does not happen, of course, and the new "plastic" Stoney society will
need to make appropriate adjustments or simply be overwhelmed by the non-
bio-degradable "benefits" of a throw-away civilization. On this front, the
Stoney tribe appears to be struggling between the two polarities of respecting
the earth and all its fullness and harming the earth by buying and enjoying
trash-producing niceties.

A harder struggle for the Stoney Indians through the twenty-first century
will be with materialism. Although many tribal members have made good use
of selected technological devices, they would not be ready to concur with their
non-Native, urban colleagues that the material world is of more value and significance than the spiritual world. Stoneys have traditionally believed that it is
impossible to differentiate between spiritual and the physical realms. There is
only one universe, and it is an inherent unity.  By contrast, modern civilization,
with its attending philosophy of materialism, is almost entirely void of any
spiritual concerns except in the form of an ever-diminishing institutionalized

religion. It is now proclaimed that phenomena that cannot be seen or felt or physically experienced probably do not exist, and in even their imagined or sublimated forms prove to be less satisfying and less relevant than things that are concrete, consumable or observable. In any activity, tangible results should be sought after that can be measured. Machines and gadgets can and should be constructed to meet every conceivable human need. Emphasis should be on comfort and convenience. In the final analysis, as some leaders of a newly-washed form of evangelical fundamentalism proclaim that God rewards in very specific terms those who obey His commands. Thus material rewards are a clear indicator of Divine or spiritual approval. Small wonder that Stoney Indians are frustrated by such words; so far their community shows little physical evidence of such "spiritual prowess."

Coupled with the foregoing is the underlying assumption in western civilization that human progress should ideally be straightforward and upward, not uneven or spiral. Decisions should be made in anticipation of future results. Achievement and progress are a natural result of an effort to master one's self and one's environment. The future should always be perceived in "better" terms because utopia is both possible and desirable. The institutional downsizing and financial cutbacks begun in the 1990s must be hard for these exponents to absorb. By contrast, the Stoney response to this doctrine is one of bewilderment. They would question the inherent assumption that progress is always possible, and, comfortingly, there are some signs in North American society that many non-Native sectors are questioning this as well. On this point the new millennium may well prove to be a watershed in which case the Stoney tradition could turn out to have been on the right side all along. Time will tell.

There is evidence to believe that human efficiency, which has always been viewed as a primary condition of human action, may have to be redefined in the twenty-first century (Knudtson and Suzuki, 1992). Until recently it was believed by the western world that if a task can be undertaken in a shorter period of time involving less people, and requiring reduced forms of human energy, such an approach should be undertaken. The appending possibly negative consequences in other sectors such as long-term effects on the environment have not been perceived as important. Untill now, the end results have justified any shortcuts.

Stoney philosophy is not known for its long-term planning. Traditionally, there was never any need for it; besides, it is within the realm of the Creator's power to do as He pleases with the earth. If the workings of the universe are respected and the spiritual implications are noted and obeyed, each day will be sufficient unto itself. "Do not boast about tomorrow, for you do not know what a day may bring forth" (Proverbs 27:1). The notion of efficiency is therefore irrelevant and it is substituted with a sense of the immediate, resulting in a temporal way of life void of any long-term plan. Take care of the earth and it will take care of you. If you take something from the earth, be sure to put something back. Taking the life of an animal to use the carcass for food requires the spiritual reciprocation of a thankful prayer. This is the purpose of striving for an enhanced personal spiritual journey, supplemented by tribal religious ritual. In this context planning for the future is irrelevant, almost sacrilegious.

To live the Stoney way is to manifest an intense and wistful appreciation for the past – reflective of a yearning that the old ways might, hopefully, return. In the meantime the lure of the "perennial now" is irresistible (Smith, 1995: 245). The essence of Stoney philosophy means yielding to the universe. Time, if measured at all, is measured in epochs, not in twenty-four hour days or sixty-minute hours. A favorite Stoney saying sums up their orientation to the universe, "When it is time, it will happen."

Eagerly we await the time when a new appreciation for the old ways – taking care of the earth, sharing with one another, and respecting all living things – will return.

# Afterword

Our culture is once again thriving. Many ceremonies are being revived with
the young taking an active part with the elders....a new culture has evolved,
a culture that had blended remnants of the past with adoptions from a new
way of life. (Pat Deiter McArthur, Plains Cree Nation, 1987: xi)

Now is a good time to become acquainted with the rudiments of
Aboriginal spirituality because the elders have declared that it is time to share
the ancient secrets (Couture, 1991a: 54). A spiritual renaissance is underway,
and the door to observing and perhaps understanding the old ways is being
opened to Natives and non-Natives alike.

The ancient teachings of First Nations posit that everything in the universe
is part of a process. In order for every living thing to fulfil its purpose, much
time will have to pass because the universe is never in a hurry. If it is the intent
to understand and appreciate the workings of the universe, and thus become a
spiritual person, one must be prepared to be inducted slowly and in stages. A
second step can never be initiated until one has mastered the rudiments of the
first step.

The spiritual world of the traditional Aboriginal Peoples was designed
around the number four which represented the four directions and the developing and functional aspects of all processes in the universe. Following the
design of the medicine wheel, each of the four directions also signified a characteristic such as connectiveness, power (innocence), introspection and models (wisdom). Each direction also featured a color, a season, a creature and an
element such as the sun, earth, night and fire. It was contended by the Sioux,
for example, that the number four is a cosmic reality. There are four faces or
ages of human beings (the face of the child, the adolescent, the adult and the
aged). There are four kinds of things that breathe – those that crawl, those that
fly, those that are two-legged and those that are four-legged. There are four
things above the earth – sun, moon, stars and planets, and there are four parts
to green things – roots, stem, leaves and fruit (Friesen, 1995a: 119).

In one sense the traditional Indian world-view posited that the number
four also indicated gradations of knowledge and maturity. Among the Plains
Cree, for example, the sundance circle was designed according to four rings.
The largest and outer ring, which had only one entrance, was reserved for

spectators. The third ring housed two sweatlodges for use by the dancers who would cleanse themselves spiritually before participating in the sundance. The second ring, a little closer to the ceremonial area, was occupied by singers and drummers who provided rhythm for the dancers. The innermost ring was reserved exclusively for dancers. One did not aspire to the inner sanctum unless one was spiritually prepared and perhaps wished to fulfil a vow made to the Creator. The sundance carried on for four days and dancers could chose to dance as many days as they wished. In a sense, the sundance was also a test of mettle and endurance.

Spectators were generally welcome to attend the sundance but they were restricted in both location and behavior. They were not subject to the regulations imposed on the sundancers, however, but could observe the entire procedure. The underlying belief was that one should not become a participant in any sacred event until one had been adequately prepared. The process of preparation required that the would-be initiate would first give evidence of having reached a certain level of maturity before being allowed to proceed to the next step.

Procedures within a sweatlodge ceremony even today follow a similar pattern revealing a crescendo of concern in the form of prayers offered therein. Four songs accompanied by prayers are offered in four segments, each lasting about ten minutes, and interspersed with breaks. The first prayer is to offer thanksgiving for a new day of life and for the opportunity of being able to participate in the sweat-lodge ceremony. It is often a general prayer that contains no petition but acknowledges the goodness of the Creator in giving life. The second prayer is a petition to the Creator to bless all people, including one's enemies, and quite reminiscent of Christ's admonition to His disciples;

> You have heard that it was said, "Love your neighbor and hate your enemy".
> But I tell you: Love your enemies and pray for those who persecute you, that
> you may be the sons of your Father in heaven." (Matthew 5:43-45a)

In the third prayer one is permitted to address one's personal needs, basically entreating the Almighty to help purify one's thoughts and provide spiritual strength for the journey ahead. If the sweat is part of the preparation for participation in the sundance, the request might be that the Creator would provide the dancer with strength and endurance sufficient to be able to complete the intended commitment.

Finally, the fourth prayer is again in the form of thanksgiving. Essentially it is an expression of gratitude to the Creator for His goodness and faithfulness, coupled with a request that those who have participated in the ceremony will have a safe journey home and thereafter live worthy lives.

In the tradition of the First Nations the teaching process attached to ceremonial instruction follows a very ancient path. The would-be initiate is taught that every ceremony has a story about its origins. Often the story is in legend form and will be told before the ceremony is observed. Two such stories follow.

In the Cheyenne tradition, the story of the Sacred Bow and Arrows goes as follows. One day a man was scouting and came up on the sacred mountain called Devil's Tower in Wyoming. Essentially this mountain looks like a huge teepee and it was once believed that the mountain had a hole straight through it from east to west. As the man entered on the east side, he saw the Sacred Pipe to the north side and the Sacred Bow and Arrows to the south. He decided to take the Bow and Arrows and walked out the west side. Since then the Cheyenne have had the sacred Bow and Arrows (Looking Horse, 1988: 67-68).

Meanwhile the Sioux became the holders of the Sacred Pipe. One day two warriors were hunting buffalo without success. They stopped atop a hill and spied a woman walking towards them carrying a bundle. One of the men believed that the woman had a message of hope for them while the other had evil thoughts towards her. When the latter reached out to touch the woman a cloud covered her and when it lifted he was found dead. The woman informed the survivor that she had something good for the people and he should return to camp and tell them that she was bringing good news. The next day the woman arrived in camp and gave the people the Sacred Pipe. She taught them how to use the Pipe and how to pray with it. She gave the pipe to a medicine man named Buffalo Standing Upright and then disappeared. As she left she changed into four animals, the last of which was a white buffalo calf (Looking Horse, 1988: 67-68).

When initiates are being readied for ceremonial induction, they are first told the origin or explanatory story. Having heard the story and shown signs of understanding it, learners may then be given permission to witness the particular ceremony as observers. Following this, if interest prevails, initiates will be permitted to participate in the ceremony and, after having done so a sufficient number of times they might be deemed sufficiently worthy to pass along the celebrated ritual. Again, the process would be initiated by relating the story to another uninformed individual and then having them observe the ceremony itself. By this careful line of procedure the sacredness of the ceremony is safeguarded, and may be carefully passed along to succeeding generations.

Learning to comprehend and perhaps even appreciate the deeper insights pertaining to Aboriginal spirituality could well follow the paradigm outlined above. Perhaps reading this book might serve as the initial step, that is – the "story" for the gradual induction to Indian ceremonialism. The second step, that of observing ceremonial life could occur as interested parties make contact with knowledgable members of First Nations' communities with a view to further deepening their knowledge. If one is sincere about learning the spiritual ways of the First Nations, it has been my happy experience that there are people willing to teach them. All that is needed is a sincere wish to learn and a genuine expression of respect for Aboriginal ways. As Joe Crowshoe of the Peigan Nation has observed;

> Some tribes say they don't want white people at ceremonies. Well, that's not sharing or communicating. The world is changing, and now is the time to reveal much of what was once considered secret. (Friesen, 1998: 62)

Since the invitation to study Native spirituality is now open and if it is enacted upon, it may be discovered that such knowledge can comprise a vital element of enrichment to one's own spiritual journey. It is an opportunity that should not be missed.

# References

Adams, Howard. (1999). *Tortured People: The Politics of Colonization.* Revised edition. Penticton, BC: Theytus Books.

Ahmed, Akbar S. and David M. Hart. (1984). Introduction. *Islam in Tribal Societies: From Atlas to the Indus.* London: Routledge & Kegan Paul, 1-20.

Barbeau, Marius. (1960). *Indian Days on the Western Prairies.* Ottawa, ON: Department of Secretary of State, National Museum of Canada.

Bear Heart. (1998). *The Wind Is My Mother: The Life and Teachings of a Native American Shaman.* New York, NY: Berkley Books.

Beck, Peggy V., Anna Lee Walters and Nia Francisco. (1990). *The Sacred: Ways of Knowledge, Sources of Life.* Flagstaff, AZ: Northland Publishing.

Benedict, Ruth, (1934). *Patterns of Culture.* New York, NY: New American Library.

Boldt, Menno. (1993). *Surviving as Indians: The Challenge to Self-Government.* Toronto, ON: University of Toronto Press.

Bordewich, Fergus M. (1996). *Killing the White Man's Indian: Reinventing Native Americans at the End of the Twentieth Century.* New York: Anchor Books.

Bowden, Henry Warner. (1981). *American Indians and Christian Missions: Studies in Cultural Conflict.* Chicago, IL: The University of Chicago Press.

Brown, Dee. (*1981). Bury My Heart at Wounded Knee.* New York, NY: Pocket Books.

Brown, Joseph Epes. (1997). *Animals of the Soul.* Rockport, MS: Element.

Brown, Joseph Epes. (1989). *The Sacred Pipe: Black Elks's Account of the Seven Rites of the Oglala Sioux.* Norman, OK: University of Oklahoma Press.

Brown, Jennifer S. H. and Elizabeth Vibert. (1998). Introduction. *Reading Beyond Words: Contexts for Native History.* Jennifer H. S. Brown and Elizabeth Vibert, eds. Toronto, ON: Broadview Press, ix-xxvii.

Bruchac, Joseph. (1993). *The Native American Sweat Lodge: History and Legends.* Freedom, CA: The Crossing Press.

Buckley, Helen. (1992). *From Wooden Ploughs to Welfare: Why Indian Policy Failed in the Prairie Provinces.* Montreal, PQ: McGill-Queen's University Press.

Burland, Cottie. (1965). *North American Indian Mythology.* London, UK: Paul Hamlyn.

Cajete, Gregory. (1994). *Look to the Mountain: An Ecology of Indigenous Education.* Durango, CO: Kivakí Press.

Clark, Ella E. (1988). *Indian Legends from the Northern Rockies.* Norman, OK: University of Oklahoma Press.

Coffer, William E. (Koi Hosh). (1978). *Spirits of the Sacred Mountains: Creation Stories of the American Indians.* New York, NY: Van Nostrand Reinhold.

Conrad, Margaret, Alvin Finkel and Cornelius Jaenen. (1993). *History of the Canadian Peoples: Beginnings to 1867.* Toronto, ON: Copp Clark Pitmen.

Couture, Joseph E. (1991a). The Role of Elders: Emergent Issues. *The Cultural Maze: Complex Questions on Native Destiny in Western Canada.* John W. Friesen, ed. Calgary, AB: Detselig Enterprises, 201-218.

Couture, Joseph E. (1991b). Explorations in Native Knowing. *The Cultural Maze: Complex Questions on Native Destiny in Western Canada.* John W. Friesen, ed. Calgary, AB: Detselig Enterprises, 53-73.

Couture, Joseph E. (1985). Traditional Native Thinking, Feeling, and Learning. *Multicultural Education Journal, 3:2*, 4-16.

Curtis, Natalie, ed. (1987). *The Indians' Book: Authentic Native American Legends, Lore & Music.* New York, NY: Bonanza Books.

Dana. H.E. (1951). *The New Testament World: A Brief Sketch of the History and Conditions Which Composed the Background of the New Testament* Third edition. Nashville, TN: Broadman Press.

Deloria, Vine Jr. (1995). *Red Earth, White Lies: Native Americans and the Myth of Scientific Fact.* New York, NY: Scribner.

DeMallie, Raymond J. (1988). Lakota Belief and Ritual in the Nineteenth Century. *Sioux Indian Religion.* Raymond J. De Mille and Douglas R. Parks, eds. Norman, OK: University of Oklahoma Press, 25-44.

Dempsey, Hugh A. (1991). The Role of Native Cultures in Western History. *The Cultural Maze: Complex Questions Regarding Native Destiny in Western Canada.* John W. Friesen, ed. Calgary, AB: Detselig Enterprises, 39-52.

Dempsey, Hugh A. (1988). *Indian Tribes of Alberta.* Calgary, AB: Glenbow-Alberta Institute.

Denig, Edwin Thompson. (1961). *Five Indian Tribes of the Upper Missouri: Sioux, Arikaras, Assiniboines, Crees, Crows.* Norman, OK: University of Oklahoma Press.

Dickason, Olive Patricia. (1993). *Canada's First Nations: A History of Founding Peoples from Earliest Times.* Toronto, ON: McClelland and Stewart.

Dickason, Olive Patricia. *1984). The Myth of the Savage and the Beginnings of French Colonialism in the Americas.* Edmonton, AB: University of Alberta Press.

Dion, Joseph F. (1996). *My Tribe, The Crees.* Edited by Hugh A. Dempsey. Calgary, AB: Glenbow Museum.

Dippie, Brian W. (1985). *The Vanishing American: White Attitudes and U.S. Indian Policy.* Middleton, CN: Wesleyan University Press.

Dixon, Roland. (January-March 1908). Some Aspects of the American Shaman. *Journal of American Folklore*, xxi:1,1-12.

Dossey, Larry. (1997). *Healing Words: The Power of Prayer and the Practice of Medicine.* New York, NY: Harper Paperbacks.

Driver, Harold E. (1968). *Indians of North America.* Chicago, IL: University of Chicago Press.

Ear, George. (n.d.). Requirements for Chieftainship in the Old Days. Unpublished paper. Morley, AB: Stoney Cultural Education Program.

Eastman, Charles A. Ohiyesa. (1980). *The Soul of the Indian: An Interpretation.* Lincoln, NE: University of Nebraska Press.

Eliade, Mircea. (1974). Shamanism: *Archaic Techniques of Ecstasy.* Translated from the French by Willard R. Trask. Princeton, NJ: Princeton University Press.

Ewers, John C. (1961). Editor's Introduction. *Five Indian Tribes of the Upper Missouri: Sioux, Arikaras, Assiniboines, Crees, Crows,* by Edward Thompson Denig. Norman, OK: University of Oklahoma Press, xiii-vii.

Farb, Peter. (1968). *Man's Rise to Civilization as Shown by the Indians of North America from Primeval Times to the Coming of the Industrial State.* New York, NY: E. P. Dutton.

Fassett, Thom White Wolf. (1996). Where Do We Go From Here? *Defending Mother Earth: Native American Perspectives on Environmental Justice.* Jace Weaver, ed. Maryknoll, NY: Orbis Books, 177-191.

Fitzwater, P.B. (1953). *Christian Theology: A Systematic Presentation.* Second edition. Grand Rapids, MI: Wm. B Eerdman's Publishing

Fort Belknap Education Department. (1983). *Assiniboine Legends.* Harlem, MT: Fort Belknap Community Council.

Francis, R. Douglas, Richard Jones and Donald B. Smith. (1988). *Origins: Canadian History to Confederation.* Toronto, ON: Holt, Rinehart and Winston.

Frideres, James S. (1974). *Native Peoples in Canada: Contemporary Conflicts.* Scarborough, ON: Prentice Hall.

Frideres, James S., with Lilianne Ernestine Krosenbrink-Gelissen. (1993). *Native Peoples in Canada:* Contemporary Conflicts. Fourth edition. Scarborough, ON: Prentice Hall.

Friesen, John W. (1999). *First Nations of the Plains: Creative, Adaptable and Enduring.* Calgary, AB: Detselig Enterprises.

Friesen, John W. (1998). *Sayings of the Elders An Anthology of First Nations' Wisdom.* Calgary, AB: Detselig Enterprises.

Friesen, John W. (1997). *Rediscovering the First Nations of Canada.* Calgary, AB: Detselig Enterprises.

Friesen, John W. (1996). *The Riel/Real Story: An Interpretive History of the Métis People of Canada.* Second edition. Ottawa, ON: Borealis.

Friesen, John W. (1995a). *You Can't Get There From Here: The Mystique of North American Plains Indians' Culture & Philosophy.* Dubuque, IA: Kendall/Hunt.

Friesen, John W. (1995b). *Pick One: A User-Friendly Guide to Religion.* Calgary, AB: Detselig Enterprises.

Friesen, John W. (1993). Formal Schooling Among the Ancient Ones: The Mystique of the Kiva. *American Indian Culture and Research Journal, 17:4,* 55-68.

Friesen, John W. (1991). Native Cultures in a Cultural Clash. *The Cultural Maze: Complex Questions on Native Destiny in Western Canada.* John W. Friesen, ed. Calgary, AB: Detselig Enterprise, 23-38.

Friesen, John W. (1977). *People, Culture & Learning.* Calgary, AB: Detselig Enterprises.

Friesen, John W. (1974a). John McDougall: The Spirit of a Pioneer. *Alberta Historical Review, 2:2,* Spring, 9-17.

Friesen, John W. (1974b). John McDougall, Educator of Indians. *Profiles of Canadian Educators.* Robert S. Patterson, John W. Chalmers and John W. Friesen, eds. Toronto: D.C. Heath, 57-76.

Friesen, John W. and Alice L. Boberg. (1990). *Introduction to Teaching: A Socio-Cultural Approach.* Dubuque, IA: Kendall/Hunt.

Garner, Bea Medicine. (1966). The Use of Magic Among the Stoney Indians. Unpublished paper. Department of Anthropology, University of Montana.

Gifford, Barry, ed. (1976). *Selected Writings of Edward S. Curtis.* Berkley, CA: Creative Arts Book Company.

Goldenweiser, Alexander A. (1968). Iroquois Social Organization. *The North American Indians: A Sourcebook.* Roger C., Owen, James J. F. Deetz and Anthony D. Fisher, eds. New York, NY: Collier-Macmillan, 565-575.

Gomme, George Laurence. (1980). *Primitive Folk-Moots.* London, UK: Sampson Low, Marston, Searle & Rivington.

Goulet, Jean-Guy A. (1998). *Ways of Knowing: Experience, Knowledge, and Power Among the Dene* Tha. Vancouver, BC: UBC Press.

Grenz, Stanley J. and Roger E. Olson. (1992). *20th Century Theology: God & the World in a Transitional Age.* Downers Grove, IL: InterVarsity Press.

Grinnell, George Bird. (1971). *By Cheyenne Campfires.* Lincoln, NE: University of Nebraska Press.

Grinnell, George Bird. (1962). *Blackfoot Lodge* Tales. Lincoln, NE: University of Nebraska Press.

Grinnell, George Bird. (1900). *The North American Indians of Today.* London, UK: C. Arthur Pearson.

Haig-Brown, Celia. (1993). *Resistance and Renewal: Surviving the Indian Residential School.* Vancouver, BC: Tillacum Library.

Hall, Terry. (1990). *How the Bible Became a Book.* Wheaton, IL: Victor Books.

Hallowell, A. Irving. (1942). *The Role of Conjuring in Saulteaux Society.* Philadelphia, PA: University of Pennsylvania Press.

Harrod, Howard L. (1995). *Becoming and Remaining a People: Native American Religions on the Northern Plains*. Tucson, AZ: University of Arizona Press.

Harrod, Howard L. (1992). *Renewing the World: Plains Indian Religion and Morality*. Tucson, AZ: University of Arizona Press.

Herr, Ethel L. (1982). *Bible Study for Busy Women*. Chicago, IL: Moody Press.

*Holy Bible*. (1984). New International Version. Colorado Springs, CO: International Bible Society.

*Holy Bible*. (1953). Authorized King James Version. New York, NY: Thomas Nelson & Sons.

House, Ernest R. (1992). Multicultural Education in Canada and the United States. *The Canadian Journal of Program Evaluation, 7:1*, 133-156.

Hubbard, David Allan. (1971). *Does the Bible Really Work?* Waco, TX: Word Books.

Hultkrantz, Ake. (1953). *Conceptions of the Soul Among North American Indians*. Stockholm, Sweden: Caslo Press.

Ironside, R.G. and E. Tomasky. (1971). Development of Victoria Settlement. *Alberta Historical Review, 19:2*, 20-29.

Jenness, Diamond. (1986).*The Indians of Canada*. Seventh edition. Ottawa, ON: National Museum of Canada.

Jennings, Jesse D., ed. (1978). Origins. *Ancient Native Americans*. San Franciso, CA: W. H. Freeman and Company, 1-42.

Johnston, Basil. (1995). *The Manitous: The Spiritual World of the Ojibway*. Vancouver, BC: Key Porter Books.

Johnston, Basil. (1988). *Ojibway Heritage: The Ceremonies, Rituals, Songs, Dances, Prayers and Legends of the Ojibway*. Toronto, ON: McClelland and Stewart.

Josephy, Jr., Alvin M. (1989). *Now That the Buffalo's Gone: A Study of Today's American Indians*. Norman, OK: University of Oklahoma Press.

Josephy, Jr., Alvin M., Jr. (1968). *The Indians Heritage of America*. New York: Alfred A. Knopf.

Kaltreider, Kurt. (1998). *American Indian Prophecies: Conversations with Chasing Deer*. Carlsbad, CA: Hay House.

Kassi, Norma. (1996). A Legacy of Maldevelopment: Environmental Devastation in the Arctic. *Defending Mother Earth: Native American Perspectives on Environmental Justice*. Jace Weaver, ed. Maryknoll, NY: Orbis Books. 72-84.

Keck, Leander E. (1978). *The Bible in the Pulpit*. Nashville, TN: Abingdon Press.

Kilpatrick, Alan. (Summer, 1995). A Note on Cherokee Theological Concepts. *The American Indian Quarterly, 19:3*, 389-406.

Kirk, Ruth. (1986). *Wisdom of the Elders: Native Traditions on the Northwest Coast*. Vancouver, BC: Douglas and McIntyre.

Klein, William W., Craig L. Blomberg and Robert L. Hubbard. (1993). *Introduction to Biblical Interpretation*. Dallas, TX: Word Publishing.

Knudtson, Peter and David Suzuki. (1992). *Wisdom of the Elders.* Toronto, ON: Stoddart.

Kodell, Jerome. (1985). *The Catholic Bible Study Handbook.* Ann Arbor, MI: Servant Books.

Kracht, Benjamin R. (Summer, 1994). Kiowa Powwows: Continuity in Ritual Practice. *The American Indian Quarterly, 18:* 3, 321-348.

Lame Deer, John (Fire) and Richard Erdoes. (1972). *Lame Deer: Seeker of Visions.* New York, NY: Simon & Schuster.

Lincoln, Kenneth. (1985). *Native American Renaissance.* Berkeley, CA: University of California Press.

Long, James. (1961). First Boy. *The Assiniboines.* Michael Stephen Kennedy, ed. Norman, OK: University of Oklahoma Press, 159-160.

Looking Horse, Arval. (1988). The Sacred Pipe in Modern Life. *Sioux Indian Religion.* Raymond J. DeMallie and Douglas R. Parks, ed. Norman, OK: University of Oklahoma Press, 67-74.

Lowie, Robert H. (1963). *Indians of the Plains.* Garden City, NY: The Natural History Press.

Lowie, Robert H. (1956). *The Crow Indians.* New York, NY: Holt, Rinehart and Winston.

Lowie, Robert H. (1952). *Primitive Religion.* New York, NY: Grosset & Dunlap.

MacLean, John (1986). *Canada's Savage Folk.* Toronto, ON: William Briggs.

MacLean, John. (1980). *Native Tribes of Canada.* Toronto, ON: Coles Publishing Company. Originally published in 1896 by William Briggs of Toronto, ON.

McArthur, Pat Deiter. (1987). *Dances of the Northern Plains.* Saskatoon: SK: Saskatchewan Indian Cultural Centre.

McClintock, Walter. (1992). *The Old North Trail.* Lincoln, NB: University of Nebraska Press.

McDougall, John. (1911). *On Western Trails.* Toronto, ON: William Briggs. Ottawa Packet. (1886). Letters of John McDougall. Calgary: AB: Archives of the Alberta-Glenbow Institute.

McDougall, John. (1898). *Pathfinding on Plain and Prairie.* Toronto: William Briggs.

McDowell, Josh. (1986). *Evidence that Demands a Verdict: Historical Evidences for the Christian Faith.* Volume I, San Bernardina, CA: Here's Life Publishers.

McFee, Malcolm. (1972). *Modern Blackfeet: Montanans on a Reservation.* Prospect Heights, IL: Waveland Press.

McGaa, Ed Eagle Man. (1995). *Native Wisdom: Perceptions of the Natural Way.* Minneapolis, MN: Four Directions Publishing.

McGaa, Ed Eagle Man, Ed. (1990). *Mother Earth Spirituality: Native American Paths to Healing Ourselves and Our World.* New York, NY: Harper.

McPherson, Dennis. (1998). A Definition of Culture: Canada and First Nations. *Native American Religious Identity: Forgotten Gods.* Jace Weaver, ed. Maryknoll, NY: Orbis Books, 77-98.

Mead, Margaret, ed. (1963). *Cultural Patterns and Technical Change.* New York, NY: New American Library.

Medicine, Beatrice. (1987). My Elders Tell Me. *Indian Education in Canada:* Volume 2: The Challenge. Jean Barman, Yvonne Hébert and Don McCaskill, eds. Vancouver, BC: University of British Columbia Press, 142-152.

Meili, Dianne. (1992). *Those Who Know: Profiles of Alberta's Native Elders.* Edmonton, AB: NeWest.

Merkur, Daniel. (1990). *Metaphysical Idealism in Inuit Shamanism. Religion in Native North America.* Christopher Vecsey, ed. Moscow, ID: University of Idaho Press, 49-66.

Middleton, John. (1967). *Magic, Witchcraft and Curing.* Garden City, NY: Natural History Press.

Miller, Alan D. (1995). *Native Peoples and Cultures of Canada.* Revised edition. Vancouver, BC: Douglas and McIntyre.

Morgan, Lewis H. (1963). *Ancient Society.* Cleveland, OH: World Publishing .

Morrison, R. Bruce and C. Roderick Wilson. (1995). *Native Peoples: The Canadian Experience.* Second edition. Toronto, ON: McClelland and Stewart.

Neihardt, John. (1979). *Black Elk Speaks.* Lincoln, NE: University of Nebraska Press.

Newcomb, Jr., William W. (1974). *North American Indians: An Anthropological Perspective.* Santa Monica, CA: Goodyear.

Owen, Roger C., James J. F. Deetz, and Anthony D. Fisher, eds. (1968). *The North American Indians: A Sourcebook.* New York: Macmillan.

Patterson II, E. Palmer. (1972). *The Canadian Indian: A History Since 1500.* Toronto, ON: Collier-Macmillan.

Pelletier, Wilfred. (n.d.) Toronto: Neewin Publishing Co., quoted in J. S. Frideres. (1974). *Canada's Indians: Contemporary Conflicts.* Scarborough: Prentice-Hall, 105-106.

Pettipas, Katherine. (*1994). Severing the Ties that Bind: Government Repression of Indigenous Religious Ceremonies on the Prairies.* Winnipeg, MB: University of Manitoba Press.

Porterfield, Amanda. (1990). American Indian Spirituality as Countercultural Movement. *Religion in Native North America.* Christopher Vecsey, ed. Moscow, ID: University of Idaho Press. 152-166.

Powers, William K. (1990). When Black Elk Speaks, Everybody Listens. *Religion in Native North America.* Christopher Vecsey, ed. Moscow, ID: University of Idaho Press, 136-151.

Powers, William K. (1977). *Oglala Religion.* Lincoln, NE: University of Nebraska Press.

Radin, Paul. (1937). *Primitive Religion: Its Nature and Origin.* New York, NY: The Viking Press.

Radin, Paul. (1927). *The Story of the American Indian.* Garden City, NY: Garden City Publishing Co.

Ramm, Bernard. (1987). *Protestant Biblical Interpretation: A Textbook of Hermeneutics.* Third revised edition. Grand Rapids, MI: Baker Book House.

Rodnick, David. (1938). *The Fort Belknap Assiniboine of Montana.* Philadelphia, PA: University of Pennsylvania Press.

Ross, Rupert. (1996). *Return to the Teachings: Exploring Aboriginal Justice.* Toronto, ON: Penguin Books.

Ross, Rupert. (1992). *Dancing with a Ghost: Exploring Indian Reality.* Markham, ON. Reed Books.

Schapera, I. (1967). *Government and Politics in Tribal Societies.* New York, NY: Schoken Books.

Schmidt, Wilhelm. (1965). The Nature, Attributes and Worship of the Primitive High God. *Reader in Comparative Religion: An Anthropological Approach.* William A. Lessa and Evon Z. Vogt, eds. New York, NY: Harper and Row, 21-33.

Schneider, Mary Jane. (1989). *The Hidatsa.* New York, NY: Chelsea House Publishers.

Schweitzer, Frederick M. (1971). *A History of the Jews Since the First Century.* New York, NY: Macmillan.

Seton, Ernest Thompson and Julia M. Seton. (1966). *The Gospel of the Redman: A Way of Life.* Santa Fe, NM: Seton Village.

Sibbald, Andrew. (inter, 1971). West with the McDougalls. *Alberta Historical Review, 19:1,* 1-4.

Smith, W. Alan. (Spring, 1995). A Cherokee Way of Knowing: Can Native American Spirituality Impact Religious Education? *Religious Education, 90:2,* 241-253.

Snow, Chief John. (1977). *These Mountains Are Our Sacred Places: The Story of the Stoney Indians.* Toronto, ON: Samuel Stevens.

Spence, Lewis. (1994). *North American Indians: Myths and Legends.* London, UK: Senate.

Stolzman, William. (1998). *The Pipe and Christ: A Christian-Sioux Dialogue.* Sixth edition. Chamberlain, SD: Tipi Press.

Surtees, R. J. (1969). The Development of an Indian Reserve Policy in Canada. *Ontario Historical Society, LXI,* 87-99.

Suzuki, David. (1997). *The Sacred Balance: Rediscovering Our Place in Nature.* Vancouver, BC: Douglas & McIntyre.

Suzuki, David. (1992). A Personal Foreword: The Value of Native Ecologies. *Wisdom of the Elders* by Peter Knudtson and David Suzuki. Toronto, ON: Stoddart, xxi-vi.

Terray, Emmanuel. (1972). *Marxism and "Primitive" Societies.* London, UK: Monthly Review Press.

Tinker, George. (1998). Jesus, Corn Mother and Conquest. *Native American Religious Identity: Unforgotten Gods.* Jace Weaver, ed. Maryknoll, NY: Orbis Books, 134-154.

Tinker, George E. (1993). An American Indian Theological Response to Ecojustice. *Defending Mother Earth: Native American Perspectives on Environmental Justice.* Jace Weaver, ed. Maryknoll, NY: Orbis Books, 153-176.

Tooker, Elizabeth. (1979). *Native North American Spirituality of the Eastern Woodlands.* New York, NY: Paulist Press.

Treaty 7 and Tribal Council with Walter Hildebrandt, Dorothy First Rider and Sarah Carter. (1996). *The True Spirit and Original Intent of Treaty 7.* Montreal, PQ: McGill-Queen's University Press.

Underhill, Ruth. (1965). *Red Man's Religion.* Chicago, IL: University of Chicago Press.

Underhill, Ruth M. (1953). *Red Man's America: A History of Indians in the United States.* Chicago, IL: University of Chicago Press.

Versluis, Arthur. (1997). *The Elements of Native American Traditions.* Boston, MA: Element Books.

Vilnay, Zev. (1979). *The Guide to Israel.* Jerusalem: Daf-Chen Press.

Vogel, Virgil J. (1990). *American Indian Medicine.* Norman, OK: University of Oklahoma Press.

Waldram, James B. (1997). *The Way of the Pipe: Aboriginal Spirituality and Symbolic Healing in Canadian Prisons.* Toronto, ON: Broadview Press.

Walker, James R. (1991). Wakan. *Lakota Belief and Ritual.* Raymond J. DeMallie and Elaine A. Jahner, eds. Lincoln, NE: University of Nebraska Press, 72-73.

Wissler, Clark, and D. C. Duvall. (1995). *Mythology of the Blackfoot Indians.* Lincoln, NE: University of Nebraska Press.

Wissler, Clark, (1966). *Indians of the United States.* Revised edition. Garden City, NY: Doubleday & Co.

Wolfleg, Mervin J. (1983). Blackfoot Metaphysics. Unpublished paper. The Faculty of Education, Calgary, AB. The University of Calgary,

Woodward, Susan L. and Jerry N. McDonald. (1986). *Indian Mounds of the Middle Ohio Valley: A Guide to Adena and Ohio Hopewell Sites.* Blacksburg VA: McDonald & Woodward.

Zeilinger, Ron. (1997). *Sacred Ground: Reflections on Lakota Spirituality and the Gospel.* Chamberlain, SD: Tipi Press.

Zentner, Henry. (1972). *Profiles of the Supernatural.* Calgary, AB: Strayer Publications.

# Index

## DATE DUE